A Kid's-eye View of the Fundamental Doctrines of the Seventh-day Adventist Church

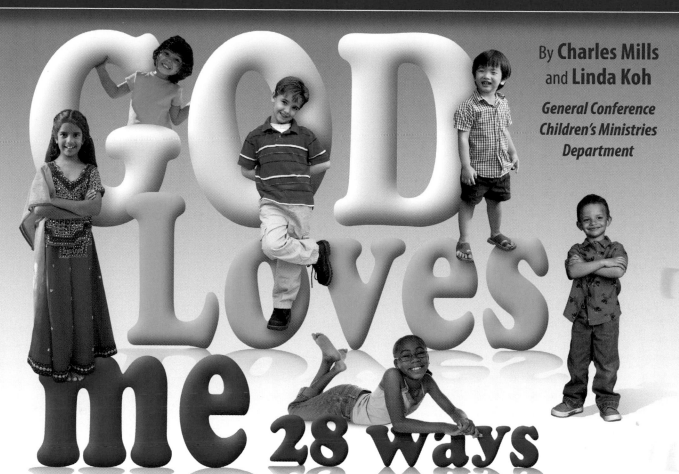

GOD Loves me 28 ways

By **Charles Mills** and **Linda Koh**

General Conference Children's Ministries Department

Pikesville SDA Children's Ministry
4619 Old Court Road. Pikesville, MD 21208
410-521-7331
www.pikesvillesda.org

GOD Loves me 28 ways

A Kid's-eye View of the Fundamental Doctrines of the Seventh-day Adventist Church

Charles Mills, Linda Koh

and the General Conference Children's Ministries Department

Pacific Press® Publishing Association

Nampa, Idaho
Oshawa, Ontario, Canada
www.pacificpress.com

Cover and book design by **Gerald Lee Monks**

Illustration credits:

Photos copyright dreamstime.com
Photos copyright iStockphoto.com
Photos copyright CanStockPhoto.com

Copyright 2006 by
Children's Ministries Department
General Conference of Seventh-day Adventists
Printed in the United States of America by
Pacific Press® Publishing Association
Nampa, Idaho 83687 U.S.A.

ISBN 13: 978-0-8163-2181-0
ISBN 10: 0-8163-2181-7

Additional copies of this book are available by
calling toll-free **1-800-765-6955** or by visiting <**www.adventistbookcenter.com**>.

08 09 10 • 5 4 3

Other books in this series designed to accompany
God Loves Me 28 Ways

Learn About God's Love **Activities Book**
by Adriana Femopase

Puzzles, word games, and other fun activities to illustrate each of the
28 chapters of *God Loves Me 28 Ways*

Sing About God's Love **Song Book**
by Kimberly Houliston, Feryl Harris, James Woods, and Janine Max

---

Fun songs for kids that will fix in their minds the Bible truths found in
God Loves Me 28 Ways

Dedicated to

Dr. Virginia Smith

who, as the first director of Children's Ministries
at the General Conference of Seventh-day Adventists,
saw the need to ground our children in the
beliefs of our church.

All Children's Ministries directors

whose concern for providing children roots
before giving them wings led to numerous suggestions
for a book to fortify our children in the church's beliefs.

All children

whose faith has taught and blessed us.

Contents

Introduction

If something is very important in our lives, we say it is "fundamental." Our families are fundamental. Food is fundamental. The air we breathe is definitely fundamental!

As Seventh-day Adventists we also believe there are spiritual things that are fundamental to our lives. Together we have made a list of twenty-eight of these beliefs, all of them based on what the Bible teaches.

Thankfully these twenty-eight beliefs are not something we have to memorize for an exam. They are not like a math problem or a spelling quiz. They are more like an instruction manual that helps us operate our car or computer. These twenty-eight beliefs help us remember what is important in operating our lives.

Over the next few pages you will read about how, through God's wonderful kindness, we can live with Him forever. You will read about the Sabbath—why we spend one day a week remembering all the good things God has done for us. You will read about why our behavior is important—how the choices we make every day can make such a difference to ourselves and others. You will read about the future and about the special messages God has shared with us through the Bible.

But if there is only one thing you remember from this book, I hope it is this—that when you choose to follow Jesus, you are choosing a life full of adventure, love, and exciting possibilities. You are choosing the best way to live your life!

I pray that each one of you will always know the secure and loving embrace of our Father in heaven.

Jan Paulsen
President
General Conference of Seventh-day Adventists

Preface

What do you believe? As a Seventh-day Adventist young person, you can offer twenty-eight answers to that question! Best of all, each answer will provide a beautiful glimpse into the never-ending, incredibly powerful, and always present love of God.

In this book, you'll find boys and girls just like you who are discovering these amazing twenty-eight ways that God loves us and shows Himself to us every day. Each lesson focuses on something you see in your own life like a simple egg, a firefighter rushing to a blaze, that old flashlight in the closet, or an empty field behind your house. All of these simple things demonstrate that God is on the job, ready and willing to bring new joys into your life.

Begin each reading with a prayer, asking your heavenly Father to open your eyes to the wonderful lessons He has for you. Then, enjoy your time with Jesus, learning of His love and looking forward to the heaven He is preparing for you.

God bless you as you discover for yourself the twenty-eight ways He loves you and all of His precious children.

1 God Writes to Me

Bible Text

"All Scripture is given by God and is useful for teaching and for showing people what is wrong in their lives. It is useful for correcting faults and teaching how to live right. Using the Scriptures, the person who serves God will be ready and will have everything he needs to do every good work" (2 Timothy 3:16, 17).

Do you love getting letters from someone you love? Are you excited when you get a letter from your grandpa, grandma, or a good friend? Do you enjoy reading every word carefully?

I got a letter from my grandfather today. He told me that he almost slipped and fell in the snow, that the birds at his feeder are eating up the seeds real fast, and that Grandmother caught a cold last week but is doing much better although she still sniffles.

Then he gave me some good advice about a kid at school who enjoys making my life miserable. I really needed new ideas for dealing with that situation. I always look forward to Grandfather's letters!

The pastor told us that the Bible is a "letter from God" written by prophets, disciples, spiritual leaders, and other men and women who were inspired by the Holy Spirit. He said God's Word tells us about God's character, His love for everyone, and His plan to save us from sin. I didn't understand what he meant until I began getting letters from my grandfather.

Now, it makes sense! God tells stories, gives great advice, and shows me how to stay away from trouble just like Grandfather does.

The apostle Paul wrote many love letters to the members of the churches in Corinth, Ephesus, and Galatia. He encouraged them to be faithful to Jesus, and he gave them wonderful advice on how to love one another in the church and in the family.

If you like getting letters, do what I do. Grab a modern translation of the Bible and read a few chapters. Begin with the book of Matthew or check out Psalms. You'll learn that Jesus died for you and is, right this minute, building a mansion for you in heaven. How wonderful that is! Think of God as a really smart grandfather with a backyard full of birds. Then enjoy your Bible—God's letter of love to you.

Check It Out!

◆ The word *Bible* comes from the Greek word *biblia*, meaning "books."

◆ The Bible was written by different people over a period of sixteen hundred years.

◆ The Bible has sixty-six books and is divided into two parts—the Old Testament and the New Testament.

◆ The Old Testament is made up of thirty-nine books and is written in the Hebrew language. They include the law, history, wisdom and poetry, Major Prophets and Minor Prophets.

◆ The New Testament contains twenty-seven books and is written in the Greek language. It is made up of the Gospels, church history, letters by the apostle Paul, other general letters, and prophecy.

Brain Game!

◆ How can the Bible help you at school when you have to deal with some nasty classmates? How can it help you in the community when you are trying to make friends? Is it easy to love such people?

◆ Find four to five Bible texts that give you some good advice about loving difficult people the way God loves sinners.

Try It Out!

Find a pencil and some paper, head for a quiet corner in your house, and write a letter to someone you love. Tell him or her all about your day, what you studied at school, or something really important that you learned when you spent time with your friends. Toss in some happy thoughts and maybe some encouragement. There. You've just written your own letter of love!

2 One God Times Three

Bible Text

"The grace of the Lord Jesus Christ, the love of God, and the fellowship of the Holy Spirit be with you all" (2 Corinthians 13:14).

"How can one God be Three?" I asked my mom after we arrived home from church. "The preacher said that we worship God the Father, God the Son, and God the Holy Spirit. Then He said there's only one God. How is that possible?"

Mother led me to the kitchen, where she opened the refrigerator door, reached in, and took out an egg.

"What is it made of?" she asked.

I'd been studying eggs in science class, so I knew the answer. "Well," I said, "it has a shell on the outside, and a yellow yolk and some clear stuff called albumen on the inside."

"So," Mom said, "this one egg is made up of three things: shell, yolk, and albumen. Right?"

God is like an egg with three parts: Father, Son, and Holy Spirit. *Three* perfect Beings joined together to make one God. One God times Three!

Now, take three colored strands of yarn—red, yellow, and blue. Braid them together into a ponytail. The three colors blend together to form a complete braid. The red color is like God the Father who loves us and forgives our sins; the yellow color is like God the Son who created the world and died on the cross to save each one of us; and the blue color is like God the Holy Spirit who comforts us when we are discouraged and helps us enjoy a happy, healthy life by teaching us right from wrong.

Remember when Jesus went into the Jordan River to be baptized by John the Baptist, that the heavens opened and the Holy Spirit came down on Jesus like a dove? Then God the Father spoke, " 'This is my Son and I love him. I am very pleased with him' " (Matthew 3:17). Here at the river God the Father, God the Son, and God the Holy Spirit were present. They work together as One great team.

Check It Out!

◆ God the Father, the Son, and the Holy Spirit form the Trinity.

◆ All three members of the Godhead love one another and have a special relationship (1 John 4:8).

◆ All three members of the Godhead work well together. The Father gave His Son; Jesus gave Himself; and the Holy Spirit gave Jesus birth (John 3:16; Matthew 1:18, 20).

◆ While God is made up of three Persons, God is united in one purpose in saving the world (John 3:16, 17).

Brain Game!

◆ If there is one God, but a team of Three, can we ask for help from any one of Them, or do they have very specific roles?

◆ Were God the Father, the Son, and the Holy Spirit present at Creation? Find some texts in the Bible that help you understand this.

◆ Jesus cried out on the cross, "My God, my God, why have you left me alone?" (Matthew 27:46). What does this tell you about His relationship with His Father?

◆ Read Paul's benediction in 2 Corinthians 13:14. Why do you think Jesus Christ heads the list in this ending prayer?

Try It Out!

◆ Clip pictures from magazines to illustrate the following: three men or women creating one business; a computer with three main parts (CPU, monitor, keyboard); a boat with a hull, steering wheel, and motor; an airplane with a fuselage, wings, and tail. Then, come up with some illustrations of your own.

3 My Amazing Dad

" 'The Lord your God is with you. . . . You will rest in his love. He will sing and be joyful about you' " (Zephaniah 3:17).

Every summer evening after my dad gets home from work, we hang our binoculars around our necks and head into the woods behind our house.

What are we looking for? Birds, flowers, butterflies, silvery fish in the pond, and squirrels. We enjoy getting out in nature and smelling the smells, hearing the sounds, and seeing the many colors waiting around each twist in the path.

I know my dad loves me because he spends time with me, teaches me important stuff about life, and listens as I talk. When I'm with him, I feel safe. Sometimes we sing silly songs or tell really stupid jokes. Then we laugh so loud we scare the animals away.

Several of my friends don't have fathers like mine. They say, "My dad never spends time with me or takes me for walks in the woods." Or they say, "My dad moved away." Then they get all sad. That's when I tell them, "Wait a minute. You *do* have a Father who loves you and will walk through the woods with you. He's called God, and He wants to be your Friend."

You see, I think of God as my *heavenly* Father. I mean, He's only a prayer away and will listen to every word I say. So, if you'd like a loving dad like mine, ask God to be your heavenly Father. Then, go for a walk in the woods knowing He's right beside you each step of the way.

When Elijah was all alone hiding from King Ahab, he was glad that God, his heavenly Father, took care of him. God spoke to him and commanded the ravens to bring Elijah bread and meat every morning and every evening. And he drank from the brook. But when the brook dried up because there was no rain, God spoke to Elijah, " 'Go to Zarephath in Sidon. Live there. I have commanded a widow there to take care of you' " (1 Kings 17:8, 9). God is a wonderful heavenly Father.

Check It Out!

◆ God is holy. That means God is perfect. He never has, and never will, do anything wrong. God has no sin (Leviticus 19:2).

◆ God is love. He wants whatever is good for each of us, and He was willing to give His Son Jesus to die for our sins (John 3:16).

◆ God is eternal. He has no beginning and no end (Psalm 90:2).

◆ God never changes. God is always the same. He was the same in Bible times, is the same now, and will be the same at the end of time. He is the same forever (Malachi 3:6).

◆ God is everywhere. He can be at two places at once—or five or a hundred and five. No one can hide from Him (Jeremiah 23:24).

◆ God is faithful. He has made over a thousand promises to us in the Bible, and He has kept every one of them (1 Corinthians 1:9). Can you find a promise in 1 John 1:9; Philippians 4:19; John 14:2; Psalm 91:14; and Romans 8:28?

◆ God is merciful and forgives. Even after we sin and disobey, God is wonderfully merciful. He is always willing to forgive you and remove your sins from you (Exodus 34:6, 7).

◆ God is our Creator. He has made the world for you and me to enjoy. The animals, the plants, and the whole universe are a gift from a loving God. The world did not come into being as an accident (Genesis 1; 2).

Brain Game!

◆ Can you identify two occasions when God was a loving Father to you?

◆ If God loves you so much, how can you share this good news with others at school and in your neighborhood?

Try It Out!

◆ Write a poem about the loving Father God. Share it with your family and friends at church.

4 Someone to Save Me

Bible Text

" 'She will give birth to a son. You will name the son Jesus. Give him that name because he will save his people from their sins' " (Matthew 1:21).

First I heard the sirens. Then what sounded like trucks roared down our street with horns blaring and lights flashing. "What's going on?" I cried, running into my parents' bedroom. "And why is it so bright outside my window?"

Mom, Dad, and I hurried downstairs and

stumbled out onto the lawn. What we saw made us gasp in horror. Our neighbor's house was on fire. Ugly flames flickered behind the windows, and black smoke billowed through the broken glass in the front door.

"Elizabeth!" I screamed. "Get out, get out!" Elizabeth is my friend. The thought that she was in that fire made my stomach hurt and my hands tremble. "Get out, NOW!"

Suddenly, the front door burst open, and a firefighter ran from the flames carrying something in his arms. Elizabeth's mom and dad, who'd been standing nearby, hurried over to him and started to cry joyful tears. "Thank you, thank you," they repeated between sobs. That's when I realized what the firefighter had done; he'd gone into that burning house to save my friend.

I hear stories about Jesus, how He came to earth as a baby born of a young woman, Mary, to save us from our sins. Wow! The King of heaven came to earth as a little baby for my sake? Yes, that night was the first time I truly understood what He did. He left His comfortable, safe home in heaven and traveled to a world burning with evil. Can you imagine that He spent three years on earth doing good, healing the sick, and teaching about God, but was treated like a criminal? He died on the cross for us. So now, whenever I see a firefighter on the way to a blaze, I think of Jesus and how He saved me from my sins.

Check It Out!

◆ Jesus is truly God and is divine. One of Jesus' names is Immanuel, or "God is with us" (see Matthew 1:23).

◆ Jesus "became flesh and lived among us" (see John 1:14, NRSV).

◆ Jesus is also truly human. He "grew and became strong in spirit, filled with wisdom" (see Luke 2:40, 52, NKJV).

◆ Like all human beings, Jesus also experienced hunger, thirst, and weariness (Matthew 4:2; John 19:28; 4:6).

◆ In His ministry to others, Jesus also revealed compassion, deep concern, righteous anger, and sadness (Matthew 9:36; Mark 3:5).

Brain Game!

◆ Is there any other way that Jesus can save us from our sins without dying on the cross?

◆ Read Genesis 2:15–17 and Genesis 3. Discuss how sin affects us today.

◆ When Jesus was tempted by Satan in the wilderness, how did He win this battle? How can you use Jesus' methods in fighting temptations in your life today?

◆ With the help of a concordance, find two Bible texts that show the birth of Jesus was really prophesied hundreds of years before it happened.

Try It Out!

◆ Spend some time at your local volunteer fire department or write a Thank-you card to the men and women who work in the fire station. Tell them how much you appreciate what they do for your neighborhood. Remind them that they are like Jesus because He saves people, too.

◆ Draw a picture of Jesus dying on the cross and hang it in your room to remind you of His love for you.

5 My Favorite Counselor

Bible Text

" 'But the Helper will teach you everything. He will cause you to remember all the things I told you. This Helper is the Holy Spirit whom the Father will send in my name' " (John 14:26).

"I'm just useless! I can't get these knots right!" I cried in frustration as I tossed out the remaining ropes.

"Come on, Jim, don't give up yet," Cliff, my Pathfinder counselor, comforted me.

"I don't think I am smart enough to finish the knots honor," I replied with a tone of discouragement.

"That is not true. Learning new things can be difficult at first. I felt just like you when I was doing my swimming honor some years ago." Cliff smiled as he put his hand on my shoulders and gave me a big squeeze.

"Hey, how would you like to learn some rope tricks?" asked Cliff excitedly.

Cliff and I soon became good friends. Whenever I had a problem, I would go to him. He always seemed to have the right words to encourage me and cheer me up. He even provided opportunities for me to excel, which developed the leader in me. Indeed, my counselor was a wonderful influence in my life!

This reminds me that I have another wonderful Counselor and Comforter. That is the Holy Spirit. In our reading about the Holy Spirit at family worship one night, Dad said the Holy Spirit works right alongside God the Father and God the Son to help us live better lives. The Holy Spirit is ready for any problem. When we're sad, He comforts us. When we're afraid, He reminds us that God is on our side and that we shouldn't fear anything. When we make mistakes, the Holy Spirit is that still, small Voice I hear in my thoughts, making me feel guilty when I sin and joyful each time I choose to obey. He lets us know what we need to do to make things better. He gives us special gifts and talents so we can serve the church.

The Holy Spirit is ready for *anything* . . . just like my Pathfinder counselor.

Check It Out!

◆ The Bible tells us that the Holy Spirit is a person, not an impersonal force.

◆ The Holy Spirit is truly God. He is the "Spirit of life" (Romans 8:2, NIV) and the "Spirit of truth" (John 16:13).

◆ The Holy Spirit is our Friend and Helper. He will teach us many things and show us what is right (John 14:16, 17).

◆ The Holy Spirit teaches (Luke 12:12), helps us see our sins (John 16:8), directs church work (Acts 13:2), and makes us pure and holy (1 Peter 1:2).

◆ Jesus said strongly that " 'people can be forgiven for every sin they do. And people can be forgiven for every bad thing they say. But if anyone speaks against the Holy Spirit, then he will not be forgiven.' " (Matthew 12:31).

Brain Game!

◆ Read Acts 2. What kind of power did the Holy Spirit give the disciples at Pentecost? Can people today still receive this type of power?

◆ How can the Holy Spirit help someone kick the habit of smoking or taking drugs?

◆ When you feel moved to accept Jesus as your special Friend, do you think it is the work of the Holy Spirit?

Try It Out!

◆ Take a little notepad and list two to three instances in your life when you felt impressed by the Holy Spirit to feel sorry for what you did, or you heard a little voice in you telling you to stop doing something unkind or make a better choice. Share this with a friend.

6 Aunt Shelly's Plants

Bible Text

"In the beginning God created the sky and the earth" (Genesis 1:1).

Visiting my Aunt Shelly's backyard is like visiting a national park. She's *really* into nature and has tons of flowerbeds, rose gardens, and brick pathways leading to tiny sparkling ponds. Birds sing in the trees, and butterflies scamper about the blossoms.

She could charge admission to her backyard and make a million dollars!

Whenever we're about to leave, Aunt Shelly fills our arms with plants. "These are gifts from God," she always says.

The minister at our church said the same thing about this earth. He preached, "The Creator made the world as a *gift* for Adam and Eve. Then, He even planted a garden just for them." It probably looked better than Aunt Shelly's backyard.

Some people insist that this world and everything in it—you, me, the animals, plants, and even the universe—came about by accident . . . by chance. They say that everything just happened or slowly evolved over time . . . lots of time.

I hate to disagree with smart people, but I believe that Aunt Shelly and my pastor are right. The Bible says that God created everything in six days. He simply spoke and *poof*, there was a horse, or a rose, or a star. Then He formed man from the dust of the ground and breathed life into his nostrils. I don't want to think of myself as an accident. I want to be a gift from a loving God—just like my Aunt Shelly's plants.

I believe that the book of Genesis is very clear. Jesus created everything in six days and then rested on the seventh day. When He was finished making the trees, animals, oceans, mountains, and Adam and Eve, Jesus looked around at all that He had done and said joyfully, "This is very good!"

Check It Out!

◆ Genesis chapters 1 and 2 tell us that God created the heavens and the earth. The earth didn't have any shape, and it was empty and dark.

◆ God spoke, and the heavens and everything in it came into being (Psalm 33:6).

◆ God took six days to create the heavens and the earth, and He rested on the seventh day (Genesis 1:1–2:3).

◆ God created us because He loves us (1 John 4:8). He wants to share the whole earth with us.

◆ In the Bible, the days of Creation are actual twenty-four-hour periods. The Hebrew word translated "day" in Genesis 1 is *yom*. When *yom* is accompanied by a definite number, it always means an actual, twenty-four-hour day (Genesis 7:11; Exodus 16:1).

◆ The Creation shows God as a careful planner. He planted a special garden home for Adam and Eve. He created human beings so they could have a relationship with Him.

Brain Game!

◆ Why does the story of Creation in the Bible make more sense than believing in evolution?

◆ What are some things around us that show that there is a God who created the world?

◆ Why is it important for us to rest on Sabbath, the seventh day of the week? Can we not rest on Sunday or Monday, instead?

Try It Out!

◆ Pitch a tent in your backyard when the weather is nice and camp out for a couple of days. Invite a few close friends to join you. Tell them about how God created this world as a gift for humans to enjoy. While snuggled up in your sleeping bag, switch on your flashlight and read a book about how to protect and conserve the natural resources God placed on this earth to make our lives healthier and happier.

When the Lights Went Out

Bible Text

"Even the darkness is not dark to you. The night is as light as the day. Darkness and light are the same to you. You made my whole being. You formed me in my mother's body" (Psalm 139:12, 13).

There was no moon when the lights went out, which means that it got really, *really* dark. I reached under my bed and found a flashlight, then went looking for my mom or dad. I don't want you to think I'm a weakling, but sometimes I need at least one parent nearby.

"Whatcha doing?" a voice called from across the room as I entered the kitchen.

"Dad! You scared me!"

"Sorry. I was just looking for the flashlight. Oh, I see you found it. May I borrow it for a minute? I want to check the fuse box in the basement." With that, he took my only source of light and headed downstairs, leaving me standing alone in the darkness.

I don't think well under stress, but an idea suddenly popped into my mind. Here I was, standing in the kitchen, waiting for my dad to get back with the flashlight. It reminded me of something we read in worship, about how God is always searching for His children who are lost in the darkness of sin. Even though we have all sinned and should be separated from God forever, He still loves His children, and He provides a way for them to be forgiven. He brings light into their lives! Kind of like a flashlight.

A shining beam danced across the wall as Dad reentered the room. "Not the fuses," he said. "Guess we're in for a dark night."

"That's OK," I responded. "God knows where we are." Dad yawned and nodded, unsure of why I said that. But, I knew why. Even though I might get lost in sin, my heavenly Father who created me and loves me will always find me no matter how dark the night.

Check It Out!

◆ Man and woman were made in the image of God with the power and freedom to think and to do (Genesis 1:26, 27).

◆ Man and woman were created for relationships with others. God said, "It is not good for the man to be alone" (Genesis 2:18).

◆ Man and woman were created to be good stewards of the environment (Genesis 1:26). God gave Adam the responsibility to rule the earth graciously and to shape it for the good of everyone.

◆ When our first parents, Adam and Eve, disobeyed God, they separated themselves from God. They felt ashamed. They had sinned by disobeying God, and they had to die (Genesis 3).

◆ All the descendants of Adam and Eve are born with weaknesses and tendencies to do evil and disobey God (Genesis 4:8, 23; 6:1–5, 11–13).

◆ Jesus Christ paid the penalty for our sins. He died in our place.

Brain Game!

◆ How can you stay away from sin at school? At home?

◆ Which part of your body system best reveals that you have been created as a marvelous being? What does that say about the Creator God?

◆ Created in God's image, how can we reflect His glory in our everyday lives—at home, at school, and in the community?

◆ Are babies born with sin? Aren't they innocent since they don't understand anything yet?

Try It Out!

◆ Visit a local cave or grotto to experience total darkness. When you're standing there surrounded by pitch blackness, repeat our Bible verse aloud.

◆ Write down one bad habit you have been struggling to change by yourself but can't. Then pray for the Holy Spirit to help you change.

8 Yellow Ribbons

Bible Text

"So stand strong, with the belt of truth tied around your waist. And on your chest wear the protection of right living. And on your feet wear the Good News of peace to help you stand strong. And also use the shield of faith. With that you can stop all the burning arrows of the Evil One" (Ephesians 6:14–16).

My brother is an army medic in a faraway country helping to care for the wounded and sick people right on the front lines of a terrible war. He sends me emails when he's not too busy and tells me about seeing bombs exploding when he goes into the battlefield to find soldiers who've been hurt.

He says for me not to worry about him, but I do.

Last Monday he wrote something strange. He asked me how I was doing in my battlefield. I told him I didn't have a battlefield, and he wrote back, "Yes, you do. You are at war with Satan." I asked my dad what that meant.

"Your brother is right," he said. "We are at war. Satan is trying to destroy our lives while God is trying to make them better. Satan tempts us to do things that will hurt us, while God, through our conscience, is working hard to keep us safe. It's called the great controversy, and it has been raging for a long time."

"You mean, I'm a soldier like Scotty?" I asked.

"Yes," Dad responded. "We're all fighting our own war. Whose side are you on? You see, God's government runs on freedom of choice and love. He doesn't believe in cheating, hurting people, lying, and disrespect (Proverbs 6:16–19). He says to love Him first and serve Him only. Then love those around us, treating them with respect and care.

"On the other hand," Dad continued, "Satan hates you and is responsible for your misery! He wants you to have fun with drugs, smoking, and alcohol. He wants to rule your mind. God and Satan are fighting for control over your life and your future. To help you overcome sin, Jesus sends the Holy Spirit and loving angels to guide and protect you."

That afternoon, I wrapped a yellow ribbon around a tree in our front yard like many Americans do, to tell everyone that I've got a brother fighting for our country. Then I placed another yellow ribbon below the first. I'm a soldier, too, in God's army, fighting Satan in the great controversy. My brother and I are proud to serve!

Check It Out!

◆ Satan led one-third of the angels to rebel against God because he wanted to have a higher position than God (Isaiah 14:12–14).

◆ Satan introduced the spirit of rebellion into this world when he led Adam and Eve into sin (Genesis 3).

◆ This great battle affects every person born in the world. Satan tries to make us do evil and disobey God (Ephesians 6:12).

◆ Through Jesus' death on the cross, God's justice and goodness are finally understood by the universe (Romans 3:25, 26).

Brain Game!

◆ What are some things you can do to fight Satan's temptations at school, at home, and at church?

◆ Can you find three to four Bible texts that can help you when you are tempted by Satan?

Try It Out!

Send emails to a soldier overseas (check with your pastor or a member of your local recruiting station to find out how). Tell him or her that you're proud of their dedication and explain that you're fighting a war, too. If the soldier's family lives nearby, invite them to church.

Stone Sermon

Bible Text

"The Lord himself will come down from heaven. There will be a loud command with the voice of the archangel and with the trumpet call of God. And those who have died and were in Christ will rise first. After that, those who are still alive at that time will be gathered up with them. We will be taken up in the clouds to meet the Lord in the air. And we will be with the Lord forever" (1 Thess. 4:16, 17).

There's somewhere I don't like to go—not because I'm scared, but because it makes me sad.

Last year my cousin Alicia died. I didn't know what to do after that. I didn't want to go to school; I didn't want to play in the soccer match. All I wanted to do was to remember Alicia because we were more than cousins. We were best friends.

One day, soon after the funeral, I was sitting in church trying not to cry, and the pastor was preaching his usual Easter sermon. He says the same thing every year, but this time—for the first time—I listened. He told about how Jesus died on the cross for our sins and was placed in a tomb. *I know just how His disciples felt,* I thought to myself. *They probably didn't know what to do either.*

Then the pastor said something I'll never forget. He said that Jesus rose on the third day so that everyone who dies loving Him can someday wake up and travel to heaven, and they'll live with Him forever. Wake up? WAKE UP? Alicia died loving Jesus!

I will never enjoy going to the cemetery where Alicia is sleeping, waiting for Jesus to return. But now, when

I see the headstone over her grave, I feel hope in my heart. Because Jesus died, Alicia can live again. And so can I.

Remember how heartbreaking it was for the widow of Nain whose only son died (Luke 7:11–17). First, she lost her husband, and then she lost her only son. Yes, the widow of Nain was filled with sadness. Life seemed to have no hope. But when she met Jesus at the city gate, He raised her son to life again! Jesus brought hope to her life again!

The apostles Paul and John died many years ago, but they are asleep in the grave waiting for Jesus to come again the second time. That will be an exciting time for Paul and John, who will be resurrected. Isn't it exciting to think of meeting our Friend Jesus on this special resurrection day?

Check It Out!

◆ God allowed His Son, Jesus Christ, to die on the cross so that we don't have to die for our sins (John 3:16; Romans 3:25).

◆ Those who accept Christ by faith will have eternal life (John 3:16–18).

◆ Jesus' resurrection gives us the assurance that He has overcome the evil forces and that we have the promise of eternal life (1 Corinthians 15:12–21).

Brain Game!

◆ What happens to those people who die without knowing Jesus? Will Jesus raise them up when He comes again?

◆ How can you share this good news with your classmates?

◆ If a friend should tell you, "I don't think I want to keep on living if my mother dies of cancer," what would you say to comfort him or her?

◆ What did Paul mean when he said, "If Christ was not raised, then our preaching is worth nothing. And your faith is worth nothing"? Read 1 Corinthians 15:14, 17 carefully and share your answer with your friends in Sabbath School.

Try It Out!

◆ Check the obituaries of your local newspaper and send a hand-painted card to the family of a person who has passed away. Show them Jesus is coming in the clouds and print the Bible verse listed with this story so they can cherish the same hope as you.

◆ Write a song or a poem about the beautiful resurrection day when you will be able to meet your loved ones who have died.

Bible Text

"Jesus went everywhere doing good. He healed those who were ruled by the devil, for God was with Jesus" (Acts 10:38).

"I'm sick," I told my mom. I don't like being sick because that means I usually have to take some really bad tasting medicine. Yesterday was no exception. Out came the bottle and spoon. Down went the medicine into my already yucky stomach. *Blah!*

That night my dad came in to visit me. I looked pitiful. "How's it going?" he asked.

"I don't know which is worse," I admitted, "the sickness or the medicine."

"Oh, but that's the secret," he said with a chuckle. "Healing is best when it comes from the inside out. If we can fix what's wrong with you on the inside with medicine that might not taste good, then you'll feel better on the outside and can get back to school and go play and do fun stuff again." Then he got that *Hey, there's gotta be a spiritual lesson in here somewhere* look on his face. "It's like sin," he said as he left the room. "Think about it."

OK. Since I'm sick and can't do anything else, I'll see if I can figure out what Dad had in mind. Let's see, sin is like a sickness. That makes sense. It can ruin your whole life. Absolutely. Letting Jesus into your heart is like taking a medicine. OK. Sometimes Jesus wants you to do things that you don't want to do such as ask forgiveness, accept punishment, or stop bad habits . . . hmm, kind of like swallowing bad tasting medicine. Hey, I got it! Dad was right! Jesus heals from the inside out and makes your life better!

At that moment, Mom breezed in with the bottle and spoon. I opened my mouth and took the medicine without saying a word. After all, I'm healing from the inside out.

Remember Zacchaeus the publican who collected taxes from people? He was sorry that he had not always been honest, and he thought Jesus might be able to help him. One day Zacchaeus learned that Jesus was coming to Jericho, so he found a good place, and he climbed up a tree to see Jesus. When Jesus came by, He called Zacchaeus to come down from the tree because He wanted to stay at his house. When Zacchaeus asked for forgiveness and decided to repay everyone he had cheated, Jesus said, " 'Salvation has come to this house today' " (Luke 19:9). What excitement Zacchaeus felt! He felt healed from the inside out when Jesus forgave him and offered him salvation.

Check It Out!

◆ Sin is choosing to disobey God, and the result of sin is death (Romans 6:23).

◆ When I allow Jesus into my heart, He helps me change from a sinner to a child of God who wants to live forever in heaven with Him (John 15:5).

◆ God's love is a gift to every one of us. A gift is something you can't buy! You can't earn it, or it would be wages. You don't deserve it. But if you believe in Jesus, that He died on the cross for you, you can have the gift of eternal life (Romans 5:15–17).

Brain Game!

◆ How can you hear the Holy Spirit speaking to you when you do wrong?

◆ If sin brings death to us, then why are people not willing to accept Jesus' offer of eternal life in heaven with Him?

Try It Out!

◆ Got a sick friend or family member? Give him or her a telephone call or write a letter. Say how sad you are that they aren't feeling well (sick people like to hear that). Then offer to pray for their fast recovery. Keep praying until they're up and about again. Then thank God for His powerful healing.

◆ Make a song about "I am happy Jesus saves me."

11 My Father's Smile

Bible Text

"[Jesus] will change our simple bodies and make them like his own glorious body. Christ can do this by his power. With that power he is able to rule all things" (Philippians 3:21).

Everybody says so—my aunts, my uncles, my grandparents, even total strangers at the grocery store. They'll come up to my dad and me while we're shop-

ping and stare at us like we're from another planet. Then they'll point at me and say to my dad, "He looks just like you!"

Dad usually smiles and says, "Yes, he does, poor kid." Then we head for the produce section.

I do look like my dad. We have the same shape nose, the same color eyes, and our cheeks puff out exactly alike. Our hair is the same shade of brown, and our chins are kind of pointy.

Looking like my dad is fun because some of my friends don't know what they're going to look like when they grow up. I do.

There's something my dad does that makes me extra glad that I look like him. He smiles at everyone—the guy collecting carts in the store parking lot, the woman at the bank, the policeman directing traffic at the school crossing, the guy who fixes our car, and that lady at the antique mall who never smiles back. Dad even smiles at my friends when we're too noisy or break something. They think that's cool.

When I fail or make a mistake, Dad does not frown at me. When I am tempted by the devil to do bad things like trying drugs, drinking alcohol, and smoking, he is patient with me. Instead, he encourages me, prays for me, and helps me to be strong again in making the right choices.

Our pastor says that when Jesus lives in our hearts, people will know it because we'll be kind and loving just like He is. He says they'll see Jesus when they look at us. Great! Now I'm going to be like two people. But, that's OK. It gives me something to smile about.

Check It Out!

◆ To grow in Jesus, you need to find a special time to pray and talk with Him. Prayer is talking to Jesus as to a friend. We want to share our joys, happiness, sadness, and struggles with Jesus and ask for His power to help us live like Him (Ephesians 6:18; 1 Thessalonians 5:17).

◆ Studying God's Word, studying our Sabbath School lesson, and meditating daily help us to become more like Jesus. It also gives us power to overcome the evil forces and temptations in our lives (Psalm 119:112; Hebrews 4:12; 2 Timothy 3:16, 17).

Brain Game!

◆ What things do plants need in order to grow? How is this similar to growing in Jesus?

◆ How did the apostle Paul grow in Jesus? With the help of a concordance, look up the book of Acts and New Testament books written by Paul, and identify the things he did that helped him grow in Jesus.

◆ How does having Jesus in your life help you overcome temptations and evil forces? Read Matthew 4:1–11.

Try It Out!

◆ Read stories about the life of Jesus. Then begin showing others the same kindness and love that Jesus showed to everyone. And don't forget to smile.

◆ Get an attractive notebook and use that as your prayer journal. Write down the names of individuals you want to pray for and the struggles they have. Then tell those people that you are praying for them.

◆ Ask your parents to buy a children's Sabbath School Bible study guide for you. Study the lesson each day.

12 *Family Reunion*

Bible Text

"You were all baptized into Christ. . . . This shows that you are all children of God through faith in Christ Jesus. Now, in Christ, there is no difference between Jew and Greek. . . . slaves and free men. . . . male and female" (Galatians 3:26–28).

There's a picture on my wall that reminds me of something important. It's a photograph of me standing with a bunch of other people taken at our last family reunion.

I love family reunions! I get to see cousins and uncles and grandparents that I haven't seen for a whole year. Everyone looks either taller or older—at least that's what my dad says.

In the picture I see Uncle Matt, who is short, so he's always in front. Then there's Aunt Sylvia, who is tall, so she's always at the back. Cousin Randy looks like he just swallowed a caterpillar (which he probably did), and Cousin Tiffany looks like she just broke up with her latest boyfriend (which she probably did). Then there's Aunt Marti and Uncle Chuck, who've been mad at each other for twenty years— according to my mom.

Some of us have black hair; some of us have brown hair. Cousin Sandy's hair is a strange orange color, and she doesn't want you to talk about it. In our family we have a doctor, a truck driver, an accountant, and a bunch of students like me. We're quite a group!

What does all this remind me of? My church! We've

got all kinds of people there too—tall, short, blonde, redhead, male, female, adult, child, policeman, shop owner, and pilot, just to name a few. We all believe in Jesus as our Savior. We enjoy worshiping, fellowshipping, studying God's Word, and telling others about Jesus. Each Sabbath is like a family reunion with one really neat difference. At church, we all have the same Father. Can you guess who He is?

Check It Out!

◆ In the Scriptures, the word *church* is a translation of the Greek word *ekklesia*, which means "a calling out." This word is used for any gathering of people called to meet.

◆ In the New Testament, the term *church* is used for the following:

1. Believers assembled for worship in a specific place (1 Corinthians 11:18; 14:19, 28).

2. Believers living in a certain locality (1 Corinthians 16:1; Galatians 1:2).

3. A group of believers meeting in the home of an individual (1 Corinthians 16:19; Colossians 4:15).

4. A group of congregations in a given geographical area (Acts 9:31).

5. The whole body of believers throughout the world (Matthew 16:18; 1 Corinthians 10:32; Ephesians 4:11–16).

◆ The church is God's family, and we are all His children belonging to this one body. Jesus is "the head of the body" (Colossians 1:18), the "head of the church" (Ephesians 5:23).

◆ We are all equal in the church. We are to love one another and pray for one another (John 13:35; James 5:16).

Brain Game!

◆ Read Galatians 3:27–29 carefully. What did Paul mean when he said that in Jesus there is "no difference between Jew and Greek"?

◆ How can you try to like people of all nationalities and colors?

Try It Out!

◆ Create a "family tree" of your church by collecting or taking pictures of members and pasting them onto a large drawing of a tree with big, thick branches. Be sure to include all types and nationalities of people.

◆ Write a card to someone in your Sabbath School who is of a different race, telling him or her how nice he or she is.

13 My Secret Club

Bible Text

" 'Many people are invited. But only a few are chosen' " (Matthew 22:14).

School can sometimes be a royal pain. Oh, my teachers are great. It's just some of my classmates who give me headaches. *Lots* of headaches.

Just the other day I was minding my own business, walking to the lunchroom, when two big guys from another grade ran up and stole my lunch box. To make it even worse, it was Wednesday. Mom always puts an extra granola bar in my lunch on Wednesdays. Granola bars are my favorite treat, and now some sweaty guy with long hair was going to enjoy my dessert.

That's when I decided enough is enough. I ran and found my two best friends, Chad and Sami. Big kids pick on them, too. Right there in the lunchroom we formed a new club, a secret club. I'd tell you its name, but it's . . . well . . . secret.

We only have one rule. No matter what anyone does to us, we won't get mad or whine or feel depressed. We'll stop right in our tracks and pray for that person. Chad and Sami have had big fellows doing mean things to them all the time, so we felt we were in a club already.

When I told my dad about what I did, he smiled. "You should call it the Remnant Club," he said. "After all, when Jesus comes, He'll be looking for people who've decided not to get mad or whine or feel depressed when people do evil things to them. He'll be looking for those who pray for others and forgive them when they do bad things. The Bible says it will be a small group, but each member will be welcome in heaven."

Then, Dad gave me a granola bar. Maybe he can join my club. How about you?

Yes, it is never easy to stay calm and not get angry, but when we do, we are stronger in conquering sin. Those who overcome sin, who stay faithful to the Bible and keep listening to the sweet voice of the Holy Spirit, will be the "remnant," and they will work extra hard to bring the love of God to the world. Though the remnant may be small in number, they'll accomplish great things for God before Jesus returns.

Check It Out!

◆ In John's description of the dragon's battle with the woman and her offspring, he used the words, "the rest of her children" (Revelation 12:17, TLB). These words mean the "remaining ones" or "remnant" (Revelation 12:17, KJV).

◆ This remnant is a small group of God's people who go through difficulties, wars, and persecution in the last days, but who remain loyal to God.

◆ Just before Jesus Christ's return, this special group has the responsibility of telling others about God's final warning to the world in the three angels' messages of Revelation 14:6–12.

Brain Game!

◆ What does the word *remnant* mean? Look it up in the dictionary to see what different meanings are there for this word.

◆ According to Revelation 12:17, what characteristics do the "remnant" have?

Try It Out!

Form a group of your own at school. Call it the "I Choose to Love Jesus Club" and invite everyone to join. At meetings each week, figure out ways to help those who refused to join or who make your life miserable. Pray for them, too.

14 One Big Noise

Bible Text

"This work must continue until we are all joined together in the same faith and in the same knowledge about the Son of God" (Ephesians 4:13).

"All right everyone," Mr. Albert called, raising his baton, "let's play!" He brought down his hand, and we all hit our first note. At that moment, we realized that something was terribly wrong. Where we usually heard beautiful harmonies from the clarinets and flutes and powerful melodies from the trumpets and trombones, the sound in our church's practice room was awful. It hurt my ears and made me wrinkle up my nose and squint my eyes. But I was playing my notes correctly. Everyone else was, too. Why was the music so horrible?

Mr. Albert waved his hand for us to stop. "So, how do you like our new song?" he asked. Band members shook their heads as if to clear their brains of the painful sounds. "That wasn't music," we responded. "It was just one big noise!"

Our band leader smiled. "You're right. And you're probably wondering why."

We nodded.

"Last week the pastor preached a sermon about unity—how we should all work together to help the Holy Spirit save souls."

"But we were playing our instruments together," I called out. "It still didn't work."

Mr. Albert smiled. "That's because I gave each of you a different song to play. I wanted you to hear what it sounds like when musicians don't work together from the same music. Now, just flip your page over to find a new song I wrote for us. It's called 'The Bible in My Heart.' "

This time, when we played, the harmonies and melodies were perfect. Why? Because we were all reading from the same music, and it was beautiful!

Similarly, harmony in the church comes when all of us are united in the body of Jesus Christ. Even though we are made up of people from different nations, languages, and cultures, we are equal in Christ. How we look and how we sound makes no difference. We're all children of the same heavenly Father. We unite as one in sharing the hope of salvation with others.

Check It Out!

◆ The church is one body with many members from every nation, language, and people. When we are united as one in Jesus, we are showing the world Jesus' unselfish love for everyone (John 17:20–23).

◆ Jesus wants us to experience unity of mind, judgment, and action (Romans 15:5, 6; 2 Corinthians 13:11).

◆ As one body in Christ, we share the same faith and hope and the mission to share the good news of love with everyone (Ephesians 4:4–6).

◆ Unity among believers is most effective in witnessing to others about Jesus.

Brain Game!

◆ Is Jesus asking us to do an impossible task of loving all kinds of people from everywhere?

◆ What steps can you take to like and get along with classmates who are different?

Try It Out!

◆ At your next family or group worship, have everyone sing different songs at the same time. Then sing the same song together. Which do you like best?

◆ Draw a nice card and write something nice to give to five classmates or church friends who are from other cultures or language groups.

15 Announcement on the Wall

Bible Text

"You were all baptized into Christ, and so you were all clothed with Christ. This shows that you are all children of God through faith in Christ Jesus" (Galatians 3:26, 27).

"What's that?" I asked my doctor as he pressed an instrument into my ear. He glanced up to see where I was pointing, then continued his examination.

"That's my medical license," he said. "Without it, I couldn't practice medicine."

"Why?"

"Because that license proves I've had training on how the human body works. It announces to everyone who comes in here that I'm qualified to help them get well."

"I wish I had an announcement for my wall."

My doctor wrote something on a chart then smiled. "But, you do."

"I do?"

"Didn't you get baptized last year? And, didn't you get a baptismal certificate?"

"Yes."

"There you go," the doctor said. "That certificate announces that you've learned something about God, about His law and His grace, and that you want to accept Jesus into your life. It tells everyone that you are qualified to help them learn more about their Savior, that you belong to His church. You should be proud of that accomplishment."

That night I put my baptismal certificate in a frame and hung it on my bedroom wall. Now, whenever I see it, I remember that I'm a Christian and have work to do for Jesus.

Many of the disciples who followed Jesus went everywhere to share the good news about the risen Savior. Hundreds and thousands were baptized. On one occasion, Philip was sent to meet an Ethiopian man who had great authority and who was in charge of the treasury of the queen of Ethiopia. After Philip explained the Scriptures to him, he believed and immediately stopped his chariot by some water and was baptized (Acts 8:38). The Ethiopian went home rejoicing. It was a happy occasion indeed!

Check It Out!

◆ Baptism is a symbol of the washing that has taken place inside of us when we ask Jesus into our lives to be our Savior.

◆ The Greek word *baptizo* means "to dip" or "to wash." So when we get baptized, we are immersed under the water (Mark 1:9; Acts 2:38, 41).

◆ When you are baptized, you are immersed in the water. Baptism is also a symbol of Jesus' death and resurrection. When we go under water, we are buried as a dirty sinner. When we get out of the water, we rise up to live a new clean life for Jesus (Romans 6:3, 4).

Brain Game!

◆ How does a person prepare for baptism?

◆ How can you influence others to accept Jesus and be baptized too?

Try It Out!

If you've been baptized, proudly place your certificate in a frame and hang it on your wall. If you haven't been baptized yet, create a certificate that says, "Member of God's Church in Training!" Include drawings of what you want to accomplish for Jesus someday.

16 Time to Remember

Bible Text

"Every time you eat this bread and drink this cup, you show others about the Lord's death until he comes" (1 Corinthians 11:26).

Do you like receiving presents? Of course, everybody does! Have you ever thought about why your family and friends give you presents? It's because they want to show you how much they love you. It is especially exciting when you get a present from someone you love who lives far away, whom you don't get to see very often.

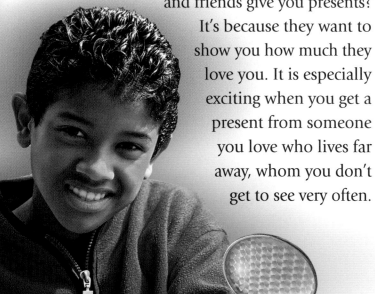

It helps you to remember them. It also reminds you that they are thinking about you too!

My great-grandfather died last year, and I missed him a lot. I laughed whenever he told me silly stories and jokes. I loved to spend time with him whenever we'd visit his farm.

Soon after he died, I got a box in the mail from his lawyer. Inside I found a beautiful pocket watch with a golden cover, shiny white face, and big, black hands. When I wound it, it began to tick, tick, tick just like it did for my great-grandfather for many, many years. He'd written a message to me and attached it to the watch chain. "Remember me," he said. "Remember me when you look at this watch. I love you. Great-grandfather."

My great-grandfather's beautiful pocket watch sits in a place of honor on my dresser. Whenever I start to feel lonely for him, I pick up the watch and listen to it tick, tick, tick. I remember the kind face and laughing voice of the old man who gave it to me. Remembering helps me feel less lonely.

Jesus wanted His disciples to remember Him too. So just before He died on the cross, He ate a special meal with His friends. Jesus shared bread and grape juice with them and told them that every time they ate the bread and drank from the cup, they could remember how much He loved them. The bread represents the body of Jesus that was nailed on the cross for us, while the grape juice represents the blood of Jesus that was shed for us.

Jesus doesn't want us to ever forget how much He loves us! He came to earth to die on the cross just because He loves you. Now He is in heaven, and one day you will get to live there with Him forever. Jesus is thinking about you all the time!

Jesus wants you to remember what He did for you and how much He loves you. Because He knows that when you do, you will also remember to tell others how much He loves them too.

Check It Out!

◆ The Lord's Supper is a service to help us remember Jesus' great sacrifice for us on the cross (Matthew 26:26–28; 1 Corinthians 11:24–26).

◆ Jesus also established the practice of foot washing. We wash one another's feet to express our need for cleansing and washing of our sins, to show our willingness to serve each other humbly, and to be united in love (Galatians 5:13; Matthew 20:28).

◆ The bread Jesus ate was unleavened. Leavened bread, with the yeast that produces the fermentation that causes bread to rise, was considered a symbol of sin (1 Corinthians 5:7). It cannot represent Jesus, the Lamb "without flaws" (see 1 Peter 1:19). So only unleavened bread could symbolize the sinless body of Jesus.

◆ The fruit of the vine must also be unfermented to represent the sinless perfection of Jesus' blood. Unfermented juice from the vine is grape juice.

Brain Game!

◆ How do you prepare yourself before you take part in eating the bread and drinking the wine at the Lord's Supper?

Try It Out!

Create a "Remembrance Box" and place in it items that remind you of someone you love. It might be a handkerchief from your mother, a baseball from your dad, a special toy from a relative, or a letter from a friend. Find something to put in your box that reminds you of Jesus. Every time you see it, talk to Him in prayer.

17 Use It or Lose It

Bible Text

"So enjoy the work you have to do here on earth. Whatever work you do, do your best" (Ecclesiastes 9:9, 10).

"I'll take it!" I said with the biggest smile my face could create. Then I placed a wad of money in the hands of the surprised sales clerk. "It comes fully assembled, right?"

"Right," the man said, slowly counting the cash. "Assembled and ready to roll."

I nodded. I had worked all summer for this moment. I'd mowed thick grassy lawns, babysat screaming children, cleaned out the shed . . . twice . . . and washed my dad's car a bunch of times. At long last, I'd earned enough, and my dad and I had gone to town so I could buy my very first mountain bike.

When we got home, I put my new purchase in the garage and gave it a quick once-over with a cleaning rag. It shone like a new coin and looked totally awesome resting on its kickstand. I sat and stared at it for a long time. "What are you doing?" Dad asked when he saw me there.

"It's so beautiful," I sighed. "I don't think I want to ride it. I just want to look at it all day."

Dad sat down beside me. "Not a good idea," he said. "If you don't use it, you might lose it. Without being ridden and enjoyed, it will rust and eventually fall apart right where it sits. It's best to use the things we have, whether a bicycle, garden rake, or a gift from God. Remember what we learned in morning worship? God gives us talents and spiritual gifts that we need to use or we'll lose them, too. That would be a real shame, don't you think?"

I jumped up and ran to my shiny new bike. "Say no more!" I shouted as I raced away. I'm going to get every bit of fun out of whatever I have, whether I bought it with my own money or it was a gift from God. *Wheeeeee!*

Check It Out!

◆ God gives to everyone in His church special gifts to use in serving others and building unity among members (1 Corinthians 12:1–11; Romans 12:6–9).

◆ The Holy Spirit provides us with gifts such as teaching, healing, preaching, prophecy, compassion, encouraging people, faith, and service.

◆ Each of us is a steward of our gifts and talents, whether it is one, two, or five gifts. We are responsible to increase these gifts by using them. If we do not use and expand our gifts, we may eventually lose them (Matthew 25:14–30).

◆ Spiritual gifts and talents are given by the Holy Spirit to help prepare church members to serve (Ephesians 4:11, 12).

Brain Game!

◆ What is the difference between spiritual gifts and talents?

◆ Can you identify two to four spiritual gifts and talents that you have? Then explain how each gift can be used in the home, at school, and in your community.

◆ Is it possible that some of us have no spiritual gift at all? Why or why not?

Try It Out!

Do you have a spiritual gift (music, writing, making people feel welcome, organization, giving speeches, etc.)? Determine to use at least one of your gifts daily and keep a diary of what happened when you did. Be sure to thank God for His generous love for you.

18 My Guide

Bible Text

" 'Have faith in the Lord your God. Then you will stand strong. Have faith in the Lord's prophets. Then you will succeed' " (2 Chronicles 20:20).

Mr. Lee always wears a hat, walks with a canteen full of water, and knows which way is north. He can identify a bird by the way it flies and tell you which mushrooms are safe to eat and which ones will make you sick. Most important of all, he knows how to take you from where you are to where you want to be.

My family and I were camping in a wilderness area where there are no roads or signs—only rough trails, towering mountains, and raging rivers. I decided to go bird watching one afternoon and got totally lost. I mean lost as in "I don't know where I am or where I just was!"

I was sitting by the path thinking when I heard something coming. I figured, with my luck, it's probably a hungry bear or angry lion. That's when I met Mr. Lee. He looked down at me and smiled. "You look lost," he said. "Would you like me to show you how to get back to your camp?"

Mr. Lee is a park ranger, a man who is used to finding lost birdwatchers. On the way to our campsite, he showed me how to figure out where I am, where I've been, and where I should be going. I listened carefully because being lost is terrible, and I don't plan to do it again . . . ever.

Dad says guides are very important to campers and to Christians—only Christians called them prophets. A prophet is someone whom God chooses to deliver messages for Him. The Bible talks about many prophets, and some of them even wrote parts of the

Bible. We can learn lots more about God by reading what the prophets wrote. But prophets weren't around just in Bible times. They are with us today, too!

In the 1800s God chose Ellen White to be His messenger. Ellen was only sixteen when God chose her. She was not a pastor or a teacher. In fact, she was not even very well educated, as she had attended school for only three years. But Ellen obeyed God's Word because she loved Him deeply, so her faith had grown very strong. She later married and became a mom too! God used Ellen White in many ways, and she wrote many wonderful books and letters to help others understand God and the Bible more clearly.

Samuel was a child just like you, when one night God called him. At first he didn't know that it was God who had spoken to him. He had to learn to listen to God. You can learn to listen to God, too! God can speak to you when you pray and when you read the Bible.

God chooses people to be His messengers because of their faith, not their age! If you believe in God, you can be a messenger for Him.

God gave us the Bible to guide us to Him, but He also gave us special people to show us the way. When you listen to the messages that God sends through His prophets, you can't go wrong. God also uses people in your life who can help you understand the Bible better, too.

Maybe God will call you one day to show others how they can know Jesus better. Are you ready to hear His voice?

Check It Out!

◆ Prophets do not prophesy on their own, for "prophecy never came simply because a prophet wanted it to. Instead, the Holy Spirit guided the prophets as they spoke. So prophecy comes from God" (see 2 Peter 1:21).

◆ Ellen G. White was one of the founders of the Seventh-day Adventist Church. She delivered God's messages to the church from 1844 to 1915. Read about her story and the other pioneers at www.whiteestate.org.

Brain Game!

◆ How do you know when God speaks to you? Read Psalm 46:10; Amos 3:7.

Try It Out!

Ask your parent, caregiver, or teacher to tell you about Ellen White. Then visit your local Adventist Book Center and buy a storybook about her life and adventures.

19 Signs Along the Way

Bible Text

"With all my heart I try to obey you, God. Don't let me break your commands. I have taken your words to heart so I would not sin against you" (Psalm 119:10, 11).

The other day as we drove to town I made a list of all the traffic

signs I saw. Here's what they said: "STOP," "YIELD," "NO LEFT TURN," "SPEED LIMIT 30," "NO PASSING," "RAILROAD CROSSING," "DO NOT ENTER," "ONE WAY," "EXIT 3B," "WATCH FOR PEDESTRIANS," and "STOP: YOU'RE GOING THE WRONG WAY."

"Why are there so many traffic signs?" I asked my dad. "After all, only a crazy person would head down the street on the wrong side, drive really fast in a school zone, or pass another car when he can't see what is coming over the hill."

"Signs aren't just for crazy people," Dad said. "Sometimes normal, law-abiding drivers get distracted or tired and aren't as careful as they should be. The highway department puts up these signs to remind us how to stay safe and arrive home all in one piece. Laws aren't just for lawbreakers. They help law keepers know what to do so they can drive responsibly. That's exactly what God's laws do as well."

"God's laws?" I asked.

"Yes. God's laws—like the Ten Commandments—

help those of us who want to love and obey God, know right from wrong. They teach us how to live when sin tries to confuse us with hurtful lies and false promises."

Now, whenever I watch traffic signs move past the car, I smile. As a law keeper, I'm glad they're there, helping me stay safe until the journey is over.

In life, I see God's Ten Commandments represent how much God loves me and how He wants me to live a happy, healthy life. Obeying the Ten Commandments is like saying "I love You" to God.

Check It Out!

◆ The Ten Commandments express God's love, will, and purposes concerning our conduct and relationships with Him and with all people (Romans 7:12; Psalm 119:151, 172).

◆ Obeying God's commandments gives us true freedom from sin (Psalm 119:45). It helps us to develop Christian character.

Brain Game!

◆ In what way can the Ten Commandments guide you in the following situations?

You act disrespectful to your mom and shout back at her.

You try to enter a football game using a "child" ticket since you're small for your age.

◆ Are God's laws really difficult to keep?

Try It Out!

◆ Paint some "God's Laws" signs and place them around your room. Make a "Don't Steal" sign and hang it where you keep your money. A "Love Your Neighbor" sign by your schoolbooks could remind you to be kind and compassionate to your class-mates.

◆ Read the latest newspapers and identify the news that shows which of the commandments were broken. Pray for two of these individuals.

20 Soccer Balls and Worship

Bible Text

" 'The Sabbath day was made to help people. . . . [Jesus] is Lord even of the Sabbath' " (Mark 2:27, 28).

It happens every Tuesday afternoon: I come home from school and Mom comes home from work. We change clothes and then do something fun together. My favorite thing is to kick the the soccer ball

around in the backyard. Or we might visit a local park, take a shopping trip into town, or just talk about important stuff like life, friends, and how to fix my hair so I won't look like a goat. Mom calls it "Our Time," and I love every minute of it.

What I like most about "Our Time" is that I've got my mom all to myself—no phone calls for her to answer, no pesky brother hanging around to bother me, no interruptions at all. Just the two of us.

Last Tuesday we visited an old lady from our church who was lonely and needed someone to vacuum her rug and fix her broken curtain rod. The Tuesday before that, we bought some ice cream at the grocery store and ate it sitting under a tree. Next week we plan to stay home and read—actually Mom will read, and I will listen. That's my other favorite.

"This is just like the Sabbath," Mom said once when we were together.

"Sabbath?" I gasped. "We don't go to church on Tuesday!"

"No," she continued, "but Sabbath is like 'Our Time' with God. We worship Him, sing about Him, and do things that will please Him. We even do it every week at the same time . . . on Sabbath!"

Guess what? Now I have two "Our Times" each week—one on Tuesday with my mom, and the other on Sabbath with Jesus. I look forward to them both!

When Jesus was on earth, He went to the synagogue (church) to worship God. He loved to read from the big Scripture scrolls. His disciples Peter, James, John, Andrew, and others went to the temple to worship God. The apostle Paul met with many believers in the church each Sabbath. It was a wonderful time to sing and praise God together and to listen to Paul preach about Jesus.

Check It Out!

◆ The Sabbath is the seventh day of the week (Saturday). God calls it holy because it was the day He rested after creating this world in six days (Genesis 2:1–3).

◆ God calls the Sabbath a "sign" between Him and His people. It is a covenant based on God's love for us (Exodus 31:16; Deuteronomy 7:7, 8).

◆ God's holy Sabbath begins at sundown on Friday and ends at sundown on Saturday evening (Genesis 1:5).

Brain Game!

◆ What does Exodus 20:10 mean when it says no one should do any work on the Sabbath? Does it really mean you should rest completely?

◆ Can you think of three or four things you could do to honor God's Sabbath?

Try It Out!

◆ Make a list of the activities in which Jesus took part on the Sabbath (the Bible mentions that He healed people, told stories, read from the Bible, shared food with others, etc.). Then pattern some Sabbath activities of your own using Jesus as your example. Be creative and have fun!

◆ Make a list of things you will do to prepare for Sabbath on Friday. Then write down how you felt when everything was ready by Friday sunset.

21 Sharing the Beauty

Bible Text

"The earth and everything in it belong to the Lord. The world and all its people belong to him" (Psalm 24:1).

I don't know how to make it grow, but I can sit on its strong branches. I can't insist that birds nest in it, but I can listen to their songs when they do. I can't cause leaves to appear in the spring, but I can spend the summer resting in their shade. When it comes to a certain tree in our yard, I can only enjoy it, even if it belongs to me . . . sort of.

When I was born, my dad planted that tree beside our house. "Someday, this is going to teach our son an important lesson about God," he told my mom. As I got older, he'd tell me about the day they dug the hole and gently placed "my" seedling into it.

That was years ago. Now, I can sit on that very tree enjoying its cool shade and strong branches. Yes, it's mine. But, it's God's, too. That's the lesson Dad wanted me to learn.

You see, although Dad gave me that tree, I can't make it grow taller each year. That's God's job. He sends the rain and sunshine. He invites the birds to nest in its branches. He moves water through its roots and leaves. So, it really belongs to *both* of us.

Oh, I have work to do, too. I protect my tree from harmful chemicals. I don't cut into it with my camping knife or prune away its dead branches in the summertime when disease-carrying bugs might get inside. I keep its roots safe by not digging in the ground around its base or burning trash too close to its branches.

Dad says I'm being a good "steward" whenever I care for something that belongs to God. I just know I'm enjoying my tree and will always watch over it just as God always watches over me.

In Matthew 25:14–28, Jesus told a parable of a man who was going on a journey. He sent for his servants and told them to take care of his things. He decided how much each servant would be able to care for. So he gave one servant five bags of money. He gave the second servant two bags of money. And he gave a third servant one bag of money. Then the servant who got five bags went quickly to put his money to work. He earned five more. The servant with the two bags of money earned two more. But the servant who got one bag of money went out and dug a hole in the ground. He hid his master's money in the hole.

After the master returned, he asked his servants what they did with his money. The first and second servants used their money to earn more for their master. But the third servant who was given one bag of money did not do anything with it. So the master was angry and took away even the one bag he had. Then the master gave that one bag to the other servants who had earned more. God wants us to be good stewards.

Check It Out!

◆ A steward is a "manager." He takes care of the things given to him by his master. How you manage your personal world is part of your response to God's love.

◆ Christians serve as managers over everything given to us by God—life, our physical bodies, time, talents and abilities, material possessions, opportunities to be of service to others, and our knowledge of the truth.

Brain Game!

◆ How could you spend your time wisely? List four or five things you could do.

◆ When God asks us to return a tithe (10 percent) of our earnings, is He asking too much of us?

Try It Out!

◆ Plant a garden or a tree in your yard and watch how God helps you make it grow. Thank Him each day for letting you be His steward as you care for the beautiful plants and animals He shares with you.

◆ Take out 10 percent of your weekly or monthly allowance and put it in a special envelope and drop it in the offering plate at church. Write down how you feel.

Bible Text

"You should know that your body is a temple for the Holy Spirit. The Holy Spirit is in you. . . . So honor God with your bodies" (1 Corinthians 6:19, 20).

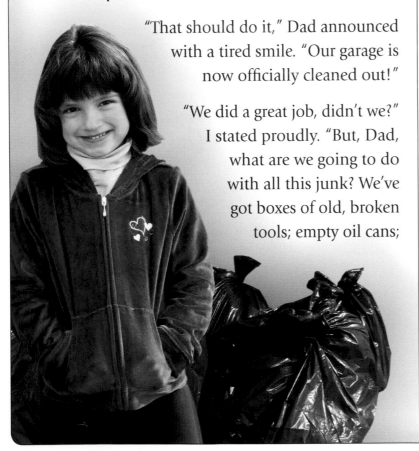

"That should do it," Dad announced with a tired smile. "Our garage is now officially cleaned out!"

"We did a great job, didn't we?" I stated proudly. "But, Dad, what are we going to do with all this junk? We've got boxes of old, broken tools; empty oil cans; a sled with one runner; and a rusted basketball hoop. Then there are those smelly garbage bags filled with dirty rags."

Dad thought for a moment, then nodded. "I know. Let's dump everything in our church sanctuary. It should fit nicely between the Communion table and the organ."

"Our church!" I gasped. "We can't do that!"

"Why?"

"Because the church is . . . is . . . God's house," I cried. "It's His temple!"

"You mean, like your body is His temple?"

"Yes. Just like—" I stopped, my mouth hanging open. "Oh, I get it," I said. "You're talking about all that junk food I eat. My body is God's temple, and I shouldn't be putting such unhealthy garbage into it, right?"

Dad nodded. "Christians should be different from those who don't know God," he said. "We should eat differently, sound different, act differently, and even entertain ourselves differently. God wants to live in our hearts, just as He wants to live in our church."

I glanced over at the trash and imagined how awful it would look piled beside the Communion table. Then I imagined my body filled with sugary and greasy junk food. Grabbing a garbage bag, I grinned. "Let's take all of this to the dump where it belongs." And we did.

Yes, Jesus wants us to live and act lovingly as His followers. Remember Dorcas of Joppa? She was a real Christian woman who was always doing good and helping poor people (Acts 9:36). Naomi loved and treated her daughter-in-law Ruth kindly even though she was not a follower of Jesus. Her loving behavior helped Ruth to decide to accept Naomi's God.

Check It Out!

◆ Being followers of Jesus, Christians should adopt a lifestyle different from non-Christians. We want to think, feel, and act in ways that honor God and to live as Jesus would live.

◆ Christians practice good health habits, for we are temples of the Holy Spirit (1 Corinthians 6:19). We need exercise, rest, and a healthful diet. We need to avoid alcoholic beverages, tobacco, and irresponsible use of drugs and narcotics that are harmful to the body.

◆ We are to apply high standards in choosing good music, books, television programs, movies, and other kinds of recreation in order to help us grow as true followers of Jesus (Philippians 4:8).

Brain Game!

◆ If Jesus lives in your heart, how should you treat friends who are unkind to you? What about friends of a different color?

◆ What advice will you give your friends at church about the kinds of books they read, music they listen to, and films they watch?

Try It Out!

Keep a supply of fresh fruit around the house so when you're tempted to eat junk food, you can satisfy your hunger with health-building apples, oranges, or grapes.

23 Ice Bag Promise

Bible Text

"Love never ends" (1 Corinthians 13:8).

The other day my best friend, Vicki, and I were sitting on the front steps of my house talking. All at once, she turned to me and asked, "If some really bad guys wanted to hurt me, would you try to stop them?"

"Absolutely," I promised. "I'll stick by you forever, no matter what."

After school the very next day, three really mean fifth graders ran up to us on the playground and started making fun of our hair, our clothes, and even our teeth. Then one of them pushed Vicki onto the ground . . . hard. "Hey!" I shouted. "Don't do that!"

"Who's going to stop me?" the bully asked, walking in my direction.

OK. Making a promise to stick by your friend forever is one thing. Actually sticking by your friend forever when there's a bully coming at you with fists clenched is quite another. But, a promise is a promise. I closed my eyes and waited for what I knew was coming.

Later that night, Vicki and I sat on the steps pressing ice bags against our swollen left cheeks. She turned to me and blinked with her good eye. "You did it," she said quietly. "You stayed. You made a promise, and you kept it. Now I know that you'll be my friend forever."

I nodded. "The preacher at our church said that married people are supposed to keep their promises no matter what," I said. "So, I figure us kids should do it, too."

If you ever decide to make a promise to a friend—or if you promise to love someone forever when you get married—be prepared to keep it no matter what. If you ever need an ice bag or two, don't worry. The hurt goes away, but your friendship can last and last and last.

Remember Mary and Joseph who were going to be married when Joseph found out that Mary was pregnant with a child from the Holy Spirit? He stuck by her after an angel appeared to him telling him that Mary was carrying the Son of God inside her. He married her, loved her, and took care of her—and he and Mary together raised Jesus, the Savior of the world.

Jacob loved Rachel, and he promised to marry her. But he had to work seven years for her. On their wedding day he found that he had been cheated by Rachel's father and tricked into marrying Rachel's sister, Leah. But his love for Rachel made him willing to work seven more years to get her. Jacob did finally marry Rachel and cared for her till she died.

Check It Out!

◆ God creates marriage between a man and a woman to last forever. They promise to love each other in happy times and in sad times.

◆ Marriage is sacred because God has made it holy. Divorce is not God's plan because we are affected by the pain when our parents break up (Matthew 19:3–9).

◆ Fathers and mothers are to love, respect, and honor each other as Christ loves His church.

◆ Parents are to bring up their children to love and obey God (Deuteronomy 6:7–9).

Brain Game!

◆ How can you help to make your home a happy and loving place?

Try It Out!

◆ Create a "Promise Book" complete with pictures or photographs. Whenever you promise to do something for someone, write it down so you won't forget it. When you keep your promise, check it off the list with a big, proud, red checkmark!

24 *Like a Rock*

Bible Text

"The Lord is the judge who judges rightly, and he will give me the crown on that Day. He will give that crown not only to me but to all those who have waited with love for him to come again" (2 Timothy 4:8).

"I'm so sorry," I said with tears in my eyes. "Please forgive me."

Dad shook his head. "I'm disappointed in you, son," he stated. "Just because your friends dared you to throw this rock through the window does not mean you should have. Besides, Mr. Miller, the man who lives here, is poor with barely enough money to buy food."

"I know," I agreed. "I made a mistake, and I'm sorry."

Standing there with my dad, I felt sick inside. I'd already promised to pay my dad back for whatever it cost to replace the broken glass. But, what hurt me the most was seeing the sad look on my father's face. I'd let him down. I'd disappointed him.

That evening, when I stopped by my dad's bedroom to say good night, I saw him kneeling beside his bed, praying. "Please God," I heard him say, "forgive my son for breaking that window today. I take full responsibility for his actions and will do my best to teach him right from wrong. Help him to see Your forgiveness in me. Thank You for hearing my prayer, amen."

Last year I learned in Bible class that Jesus is busy right now, deciding who will go with Him to heaven when He returns to earth the second time. The teacher read that Jesus will forgive anyone who asks with a sincere heart. My dad showed me how it works; Jesus forgives and then, through the Holy Spirit, He teaches, just like my father forgives and teaches me.

God instructed Moses and the children of Israel to build a temple in the wilderness to explain what Jesus is doing right now in heaven. In the wilderness, the priests oversaw the forgiveness of sins and the judgment of those who chose to do evil. That's what Jesus is doing right now in heaven. He is our heavenly Priest waiting to forgive us, clean sin from our lives, and finally welcome us home to heaven.

So on my dresser rests a rock, a reminder that Jesus wants to forgive my every sin, show me right from wrong, and someday take me home to heaven with Him. Wow! Jesus loves me, just like my dad!

Check It Out!

◆ There is a sanctuary, or temple, in heaven. It is the dwelling place of God (Revelation 4:1–4).

◆ Jesus is our High Priest serving on our behalf in the heavenly temple (Hebrews 8:1, 2).

Brain Game!

◆ If I confess my sins to Jesus, He will forgive me. But what about those sins I have forgotten to confess? Will He still forgive me?

◆ How do you feel when someone you have wronged forgives you?

Try It Out!

◆ Make a judge's gavel out of wood and place it on your dresser. After you pray and ask God to forgive your sins, pick up the gavel, tap it on the dresser, and say, "Forgiven!"

◆ Get a little notebook or prayer journal. Write down the wrong things you have done each day, and then at the end of the day, ask God to forgive all your sins. Then using a red marker, make a red cross over the page that lists your sins and write the word "Forgiven."

25 Red Minivan

Bible Text

"Look, Jesus is coming with the clouds! Everyone will see him. . . . Yes, this will happen!" (Revelation 1:7, 8).

I don't have time to talk. My grandparents are coming, and the house is a mess! They come only twice a year, and we want everything to be perfect. I've vacuumed the downstairs rug, dusted the furniture—including the knick-knacks on the mantle, which are a real chore—and helped my mom wash the sheets.

Dad is outside mowing the lawn, and my brother is in his room playing on his computer. I think he's supposed to be washing the dishes, but he never lets responsibility and hard work get in the way of his fun.

We've got fresh flowers in all the vases, Grandfather's favorite food—potato salad and fresh corn on the cob—in the refrigerator, and there's a cherry pie cooling on the counter. I know my grandmother likes fruit, so there are shiny apples in the big bowl on the dining room table.

I even bought a new pair of jeans to wear when they get here. This is going to be great!

Whenever my grandparents come, we really make the place sparkle. We plan things we know they'll enjoy—like taking walks down by the river or visiting the local history museum. We watch excitedly for their little red minivan.

Dad says waiting for their little red minivan to arrive is kind of like waiting for Jesus to return. Both require a lot of preparation. Jesus is going to return to this earth and invite everyone who has chosen to love and obey Him to heaven (John 14:1–4). When He comes, those who hate Him will be destroyed. But everyone else, even the faithful who have died in the past, will leave this dark world and spend eternity with Jesus. So, if your grandparents aren't on their way, Jesus is! You'd better get busy. And make sure your brother is ready to meet Him, too!

Check It Out!

◆ Jesus told His disciples that He would be returning to His Father to prepare a place for them. He promised, " 'I will come again' " (John 14:3, NKJV).

◆ Jesus' return will be very visible. "He is coming with clouds" (Revelation 1:7, NKJV).

◆ Jesus' return will be very loud. "The Lord Himself will descend from heaven with a shout, with the voice of an archangel, and with the trumpet of God" (1 Thessalonians 4:16, NKJV).

◆ Jesus Christ will come as a conqueror, with power and glory (Matthew 16:27). John the Revelator pictures Jesus riding on a white horse and leading the numerous armies of heaven (Revelation 19:11–16).

◆ Jesus Christ's second coming will be witnessed by the righteous and the wicked, and every eye will see Him (Revelation 1:7).

◆ No one knows the exact day when Jesus will return the second time (Matthew 24:36). So we need to be ready at all times.

Brain Game!

◆ How can you be prepared each day for Jesus to come? Don't you still have to go to school, do homework, etc.?

◆ How can you help your friends to be ready for Jesus to come?

◆ Can you identify some signs of Jesus' coming as listed in Matthew 24? Are you seeing any of these signs being fulfilled?

Try It Out!

◆ Create a list of the things you'd do if you knew Jesus was coming today. What would you change in your life? What would you stop doing? What would you start doing? Then begin working on all the items on your list, thanking God for His soon return.

◆ Visit a senior citizen home or a children's home and share with the people there the good news that Jesus is coming again.

26 Field of Dreams

Bible Text

"The Lord himself will come down from heaven. There will be a loud command with the voice of the archangel and with the trumpet call of God. And those who have died and were in Christ will rise first" (1 Thessalonians 4:16).

"I don't understand," I said. "My friend, Danny, is dead. We placed his coffin in the ground, and then those men covered it up with soil. But the preacher stood right there by the gravesite and told everyone that we'll see Danny again when Jesus comes. How is that possible?"

My mom put her hand on my shoulder. "Let's go for a walk," she invited.

We strolled to a large field behind our house and sat down on a fallen log. "What do you see out there?" she asked, pointing.

"I see green grass and lots of spring flowers," I responded, enjoying the colorful display.

"What did you see out there last winter?"

"Oh," I said with a shake of my head, "I saw brown earth, ice, and tons of snow."

"What happened?" Mom wanted to know. "What made the change?"

I shrugged. "Spring, I guess. When spring came, the snow and ice melted, and the grass and flowers popped out of the ground." I paused as a new, exciting thought filled my mind. "The grass and flowers were waiting in the ground, waiting for the sunshine and the rain, for the warm breezes to blow, for . . . for . . . life!"

Mom smiled. "Think of the coming resurrection as a big, joyous springtime. Only it won't be the sun or rain that will be calling grasses from the ground; it will be Jesus calling out the names of everyone who has died loving and trusting Him. People . . . like Danny."

I gazed out over the beautiful field and nodded. Now I understood, and suddenly I felt hopeful inside.

Remember how sad Mary and Martha were after their brother Lazarus had died? Several days before, they had sent someone to tell Jesus so that He could come and heal their brother. But Jesus did not come immediately. However, when He did come, Jesus told Martha not to be sad, for " 'Your brother will rise and live again' " (John 11:23).

How could it be? Martha was puzzled, for she knew that Lazarus would rise again only in the resurrection at the last day. But Jesus' words brought great comfort and hope to Martha, Mary, and all those who love Him. Jesus said, " 'I am the resurrection and the life. He who believes in me will have life even if he dies' " (John 11:25). Oh, yes, Jesus will call us up from the grave when He comes again.

Check It Out!

◆ All who have sinned and disobeyed God will die. But death is like a sleep (Matthew 9:24; John 11:11–14).

◆ When Jesus returns, all those who have loved Him and have died will rise up out of their graves to meet Him in the air (John 5:28, 29).

◆ Those who are saved will travel to heaven to spend the next one thousand years (the millennium) with Jesus.

◆ The wicked and unrighteous dead will be raised at the end of the one thousand years.

Brain Game!

◆ How can you share this comforting news with friends or classmates who have just lost someone special?

◆ What happens when a person dies? Read Ecclesiastes 9:5, 6.

Try It Out!

◆ Plant your own "field of dreams" in a small plot of earth by your house. Each spring, when you watch the flowers pop up, thank God for the coming resurrection.

27 Burn Barrel

Bible Text

"[God] will wipe away every tear from their eyes. There will be no more death, sadness, crying, or pain. All the old ways are gone" (Revelation 21:4).

"Be careful," Dad called as he raked up another large pile of dead leaves. "Don't get too close. I wouldn't want you to singe your eyebrows."

I laughed as the flames in our big backyard burn barrel consumed the last load I'd tossed in. "I'd look pretty funny without eyebrows," I called back. "Just keep those leaves coming. We'll have the entire yard cleaned up by lunchtime."

As I stood there watching the leaves vanish in the fire, I got to thinking about something I'd read a few days before. The Bible says that right before we live forever with God in the new earth, He will destroy evil. It says the whole world will suddenly become like one great, big lake of fire. Pain, suffering, and everything bad will vanish into it just like my dried leaves.

While I'm sure God won't enjoy seeing the people who refuse to love and trust Him turn away and choose the fire over heaven, some parts of that awful event sound exciting.

I picked up a wrinkled oak leaf. "You are all the diseases in the world," I told it. Then I tossed it into the burn barrel. *Poof.* It vanished! Grabbing another leaf, I announced, "You are fear." Into the fire it went. *Poof.*

Gone! *Hey, this is great,* I thought. "You are lying and cheating," I told the next leaf. Gone! "You are pain, hurt, and worry," I told another. *Poof!* Taking hold of a very large leaf, I announced firmly, "You are death!" It vanished without a trace.

"Why are you burning our leaves one at a time?" Dad asked.

"Oh, I'm just doing something like God's going to do someday," I said as Dad brought me another pile. Into the burn barrel it went, never to litter our yard again.

Check It Out!

◆ During the one thousand years (the millennium), those who are saved will live with Jesus Christ (Revelation 20:1–4).

◆ This isn't a judgment of who's saved and who's lost. Each of us will have made our personal choices before Jesus comes.

◆ During the millennium Satan has no one to tempt because the brightness of Jesus' coming has destroyed the living who weren't trusting in Him, and the rest of the dead just slept on (Revelation 20:2, 3).

◆ At the end of the one thousand years, the wicked dead will be resurrected, and fire from God will destroy them as well as Satan and his angels. The earth will be cleansed (Revelation 20:5, 9).

Brain Game!

◆ How can each of us prepare to live with Jesus?

◆ How can you say No to Satan each day so you can be with Jesus?

Try It Out!

If you have a burn barrel or fireplace where you live, write down on pieces of paper the sins and temptations you fight every day and toss them into the flames. Think about the joy that will fill God's heart when He erases sin and suffering from this world forever.

Bible Text

" ' "*But the saints of the Most High will receive the kingdom and will possess it forever—yes, for ever and ever*" ' " (Daniel 7:18, NIV).

"That's the strangest clock I've ever seen," I said to Mr. Chira, owner of the little antique shop on Main Street in our town.

Mr. Chira smiled. "I know what you mean. It doesn't have any hands. They probably got lost a long time ago. I bought it because it teaches me something about heaven."

"What?" I asked.

Mr. Chira came over and stood beside me. "My family and I are looking forward to living in heaven, just as I know you and your family are, too. We'll all enjoy playing with the totally friendly animals, eating the delicious fruit from the tree of life, flying like rocket ships to faraway solar systems, and visiting with Jesus. That old clock reminds me that we'll be able to do those wonderful, thrilling, and exhilarating activities *forever*. Why? Because there is no time in heaven; no clocks, no schedules. Just unhurried peace and joy."

"Sounds nice," I said, catching a bit of Mr. Chira's excitement. "No appointments to keep," I mused, "unless you promised a bear you'd meet him by the river after supper. And you'll never be late to anything either because there's—"

"No time," Mr. Chira sighed with a grin. "Just forever fun. Isn't that great?"

I glanced at the clock with no hands and nodded. "I gotta get me one of those."

"Here," my friend said with a smile. "Take this one

home as a gift. Think about heaven whenever you see it."

That old handless clock now rests on my nightstand. Whenever I glance at it, I wonder what it will be like to live in a land where there's only time for joy. I can hardly wait!

Check It Out!

◆ When Satan and sinners are gone, our heavenly Father will create a brand-new world for us to enjoy.

◆ After the one thousand years (millennium), the Holy City, the New Jerusalem, will come down to the earth and God will make His home with the saved forever.

◆ In the Hebrew language, *Jerusalem* means "city of peace."

◆ The new earth will be a beautiful place because God and Jesus will be there.

◆ The great controversy will be ended, and there will be no more sin or sinners.

◆ All who love God will enjoy this wonderful world forever and ever with God (Revelation 11:15).

Brain Game!

◆ What questions would you like to ask God and Jesus in the new earth? List several.

◆ What are some special things you would like to do in the new earth that you can't do now?

Try It Out!

Find an old clock and remove the hour, minute, and second hands. Place it where you'll see it every day. You, too, can look forward to living forever in a time-less land.

God Loves Me 28 Ways Beliefs

by Charles Mills

1. The Word of God

I believe that God inspired every writer whose words appear in the Bible. Everything they wrote is true, and what they said can help me live a happy and healthy life.

2. The Godhead

I believe that the God who loves me is actually Three Gods in One—the Father, the Son, and the Holy Spirit. Each works hard to teach me how to live a better, more meaningful life.

3. God the Father

I believe that God the Father is the power that keeps me—and every other creature in the universe—alive. He is kind and forgiving, and will never leave me alone.

4. God the Son

I believe that God the Son, Jesus, created this world and everything good in it. Two thousand years ago, He came to this earth as a baby, grew up and lived a sinless life, then died on the cross so that I could some-day live forever with Him in heaven.

5. God the Holy Spirit

I believe that God the Holy Spirit is that still, small Voice I hear in my thoughts whenever I feel afraid, sad, or lonely. It tells me that everything will be all right. The Holy Spirit also tries to teach me right from wrong by making me feel guilty when I sin and joyful each time I choose to obey God's laws of love.

6. Creation

I believe that Jesus created everything in six days and then rested on the seventh day. When He was finished making the trees, animals, oceans, mountains, and Adam and Eve, Jesus looked around at all that He had done and said joyfully, "This is very good!"

7. The Nature of Man

I believe that Jesus made people in the image of God. Each enjoys the freedom to think and act any way they want. Even though sin and bad choices have brought pain and suffering to many, we're still children of God. With the help of the Holy Spirit, we can care for each other just like God cares for each one of us.

8. The Great Controversy

I believe that Satan is a real being who wants to destroy us all. He works hard each day to bring destructive sin into our lives. God wants us to live each day with joy, happiness, and love. God and Satan are fighting for control over our lives and our futures. To help us overcome sin, Jesus sends the Holy Spirit and loving angels to guide and protect us.

9. Life, Death, and Resurrection of Jesus

I believe that Jesus lived a perfect life in order to show us that it's possible to overcome sin. He died on the cross so I won't have to lose my heavenly home because of my sins. Then, God raised Jesus from the dead to demonstrate how He'll someday raise me from the dead if I die before Jesus returns.

10. The Experience of Salvation

I believe that when I allow Jesus into my heart, He helps me change from a sinner to a child of God, ready to live forever in heaven. He teaches me how to be like Him as I read my Bible and follow the loving guidance of the Holy Spirit. Thanks to Jesus, I can be confident that I'm forgiven and that there's a home waiting for me in heaven.

11. Growing in Jesus

I believe that when someone invites Jesus into his or her heart, changes start to happen fast. What that person reads, watches on television or on the Internet, eats and listens to; the places he or she goes; even the words they say will change. The pages of the Bible will become like a textbook for living, and many whispered prayers will come from their lips. These changes keep happening, day after day, until Jesus comes.

12. The Church

I believe that my church is a place where people who love Jesus can praise Him together without fear or embarrassment. It's like attending a fun family reunion each week. Jesus loves His church and listens to every word spoken and every song sung.

13. The Remnant and Its Mission

I believe that before Jesus comes the second time, some people in my church will choose sin over salvation. Those who stay faithful to the Bible and keep listening to the sweet voice of the Holy Spirit are called the remnant, and they will work extra hard to bring the love of God to the world. Though the remnant may be small in number, they'll accomplish great things for God so that Jesus can return.

14. Unity in the Body of Christ

I believe that any church whose members worship God should welcome people from any nation, who speak any language, and whose skin is any color. We're all equal in God's sight. How we look and how we sound makes no difference. We're all children of the same heavenly Father.

15. Baptism

I believe that when I'm baptized, I'm telling everyone that I love God and want to live my life in service to Him. Baptism is like being buried as a dirty sinner and then rising up to live a new, clean life for Jesus.

16. The Lord's Supper

I believe that when Jesus ate His last meal with His disciples right before He was crucified, He taught us something wonderful. He said that the grape juice (wine) represented His spilled blood and that the bread represented His broken body. When I eat "The Lord's Supper" at church, it helps me remember the sacrifice Jesus made for me on the cross.

17. Spiritual Gifts and Ministries

I believe that God has given me (and you) special talents that we can use to serve Him. We each enjoy different skills like music, preaching, teaching, art, giving Bible studies, visiting the sick, or making people feel welcome when they visit our church. Each spiritual gift is important to the work of God.

18. The Gift of Prophecy

I believe that the people in God's church need help knowing how to live and what to look forward to in the future. So, God invited a woman named Ellen G. White to be His prophet and provide guidance, instruction, and correction for His people. She also helps us understand the important lessons found in the Bible. When I read what God's prophet wrote a long time ago, I'm discovering important things that God wants to say to me today.

19. The Law of God

I believe that God's Ten Commandments contain the best rules for living. Each is designed to protect me from sin and help me stay out of trouble. Each represents how much God loves me and how He wants me to live a happy, healthy life. Obeying the Ten Commandments is like saying "I love You" to God.

20. The Sabbath

I believe that God created the seventh day (Saturday) to be a holy day. He commands me to do special work for Him on that day as a way of showing Him—and others—that I believe He is the Creator of all good things. God's holy Sabbath begins at sundown on Friday and ends at sundown on Saturday.

21. Stewardship

I believe that everything belongs to God, the trees, the flowers, the animals—even me. God has asked me to take care of what He created and to protect all things from harm—even me. So, I will cherish God's creatures and creation. To show Him how proud I am to be His steward, I'll faithfully return a tithe (10 percent) of my time, talent, and money. I want God to bless this world and everything in it—even me.

22. Christian Behavior

I believe that anyone who loves Jesus should talk, act, eat, work, and play differently from those who love Satan. Everything I do should show others that Jesus lives in my heart and that I'm doing my best to live by His rules of love.

23. Marriage and the Family

I believe that in order for us to understand the joy of living in heaven, God invites us to create families here on this earth. When we love our brothers and sisters, uncles and aunts, parents and grandparents, we're experiencing a beautiful example of what it will be like to live in heaven with everyone who has chosen to love and obey God. Our heavenly Father wants our earthly homes to be safe places to learn about His love and forgiveness.

24. Jesus' Ministry in the Heavenly Sanctuary

I believe that God instructed Moses and the children of Israel to build a temple in the wilderness to explain what Jesus is doing right now in heaven. In the wilderness, the priests oversaw the forgiveness of sins and the judgment of those who chose to do evil. That's what Jesus is doing right now in heaven. He is our heavenly Priest waiting to forgive us, clean sin from our hearts, and finally welcome us home to heaven.

25. The Second Coming of Jesus

I believe that, one day soon, Jesus is going to return to this earth and invite everyone who has chosen to love and obey Him to heaven. When He comes, those who hate Him will be destroyed. But everyone else, even the faithful who have died in the past, will leave this dark world and spend eternity with Jesus.

26. Death and Resurrection

I believe that Jesus can raise people from the dead. He did it before (like Lazarus and the widow's son), and He will do it again when He returns the second time. So, even though some of my family sleep in the ground, I'll see them again because of the power of God over death.

27. The Millennium and the End of Sin

I believe that, someday, sin and sinners will be gone forever. My Bible says that even those who died hating God will fully understand the lies that Satan told them and will agree that God's judgment is just. Without God's presence to shield them from harm, Satan and every sinner will face the world alone and be completely destroyed by fire.

28. The New Earth

I believe that when Satan and sinners are gone, my heavenly Father will create a brand-new world for us to enjoy. There will be no death, no tears, no pain, no suffering. All will be peace and love. Best of all, I, my family, and all who love God will enjoy this wonderful world forever and ever.

Fundamental Beliefs
of the Seventh-day Adventist Church

Seventh-day Adventists accept the Bible as their only creed and hold certain fundamental beliefs to be the teachings of the Holy Scriptures. These beliefs, as set forth here, constitute the church's understanding and expression of the teaching of Scripture. Revision of these statements may be expected at a General Conference session when the church is led by the Holy Spirit to a fuller understanding of Bible truths or finds better language to express the teachings of God's Holy Word.

1. The Holy Scriptures

The Holy Scriptures, Old and New Testaments, are the written Word of God, given by divine inspiration through holy men of God who spoke and wrote as they were moved by the Holy Spirit. In this Word, God has committed to man the knowledge necessary for salvation. The Holy Scriptures are the infallible revelation of His will. They are the standard of character, the test of experience, the authoritative revealer of doctrines, and the trustworthy record of God's acts in history.

(2 Pet. 1:20, 21; 2 Tim. 3:16, 17; Ps. 119:105; Prov. 30:5, 6; Isa. 8:20; John 17:17; 1 Thess. 2:13; Heb. 4:12.)

2. The Trinity

There is one God: Father, Son, and Holy Spirit, a unity of three co-eternal Persons. God is immortal, all-powerful, all-knowing, above all, and ever present. He is infinite and beyond human comprehension, yet known through His self-revelation. He is forever worthy of worship, adoration, and service by the whole creation.

(Deut. 6:4; Matt. 28:19; 2 Cor. 13:14; Eph. 4:4–6; 1 Pet. 1:2; 1 Tim. 1:17; Rev. 14:7.)

3. The Father

God the eternal Father is the Creator, Source, Sustainer, and Sovereign of all creation. He is just and holy, merciful and gracious, slow to anger, and abounding in steadfast love and faithfulness. The qualities and powers exhibited in the Son and the Holy Spirit are also revelations of the Father.

(Gen. 1:1; Rev. 4:11; 1 Cor. 15:28; John 3:16; 1 John 4:8; 1 Tim. 1:17; Exod. 34:6, 7; John 14:9.)

4. The Son

God the eternal Son became incarnate in Jesus Christ. Through Him all things were created, the character of God is revealed, the salvation of humanity is accomplished, and the world is judged. Forever truly God, He became also truly man, Jesus the Christ. He was conceived of the Holy Spirit and born of the virgin Mary. He lived and experienced temptation as a human being, but perfectly exemplified the righteousness and love of God. By His miracles He manifested God's power and was attested as God's promised Messiah. He suffered and died voluntarily on the cross for our sins and in our place, was raised from the dead, and ascended to minister in the heavenly sanctuary in our behalf. He will come again in glory for the final deliverance of His people and the restoration of all things.

(John 1:1–3, 14; Col. 1:15–19; John 10:30; 14:9; Rom. 6:23; 2 Cor. 5:17–19; John 5:22; Luke 1:35; Phil. 2:5–11; Heb. 2:9–18; 1 Cor. 15:3, 4; Heb. 8:1, 2; John 14:1–3.)

5. The Holy Spirit

God the eternal Spirit was active with the Father and the Son in Creation, incarnation, and redemption. He inspired the writers of Scripture. He filled Christ's life with power. He draws and convicts human beings; and those who respond He renews and transforms into the image of God. Sent by the Father and the Son to be always with His children, He extends spiritual gifts to the church, empowers it to bear witness to Christ, and in harmony with the Scriptures leads it into all truth.

(Gen. 1:1, 2; Luke 1:35; 4:18; Acts 10:38; 2 Pet. 1:21; 2 Cor. 3:18; Eph. 4:11, 12; Acts 1:8; John 14:16–18, 26; 15:26, 27; 16:7–13.)

6. Creation

God is Creator of all things, and has revealed in Scripture the authentic account of His creative activity. In six days the Lord made "the heaven and the earth" and all living things upon the earth, and rested on the seventh day of that first week. Thus He established the Sabbath as a perpetual memorial of His completed creative work. The first man and woman were made in the image of God as the crowning work of Creation, given dominion over the world, and charged with responsibility to care for it. When the world was finished it was "very good," declaring the glory of God.

(Gen. 1; 2; Exod. 20:8–11; Pss. 19:1–6; 33:6, 9; 104; Heb. 11:3.)

7. The Nature of Man

Man and woman were made in the image of God with individuality, the power and freedom to think and to do. Though created free beings, each is an indivisible unity of body, mind, and spirit, dependent upon God for life and breath and all else. When our first parents disobeyed God, they denied their dependence upon Him and fell from their high position under God. The image of God in them was marred and they became subject to death. Their descendants share this fallen nature and its consequences. They are born with weaknesses and tendencies to evil. But God

in Christ reconciled the world to Himself and by His Spirit restores in penitent mortals the image of their Maker. Created for the glory of God, they are called to love Him and one another, and to care for their environment.

(Gen. 1:26–28; 2:7; Ps. 8:4–8; Acts 17:24–28; Gen. 3; Ps. 51:5; Rom. 5:12–17; 2 Cor. 5:19, 20; Ps. 51:10; 1 John 4:7, 8, 11, 20; Gen. 2:15.)

8. The Great Controversy

All humanity is now involved in a great controversy between Christ and Satan regarding the character of God, His law, and His sovereignty over the universe. This conflict originated in heaven when a created being, endowed with freedom of choice, in self-exaltation became Satan, God's adversary, and led into rebellion a portion of the angels. He introduced the spirit of rebellion into this world when he led Adam and Eve into sin. This human sin resulted in the distortion of the image of God in humanity, the disordering of the created world, and its eventual devastation at the time of the worldwide flood. Observed by the whole creation, this world became the arena of the universal conflict, out of which the God of love will ultimately be vindicated. To assist His people in this controversy, Christ sends the Holy Spirit and the loyal angels to guide, protect, and sustain them in the way of salvation.

(Rev. 12:4–9; Isa. 14:12–14; Ezek. 28:12-18; Gen. 3; Rom. 1:19–32; 5:12–21; 8:19–22; Gen. 6–8; 2 Pet. 3:6; 1 Cor. 4:9; Heb. 1:14.)

9. The Life, Death, and Resurrection of Christ

In Christ's life of perfect obedience to God's will, His suffering, death, and resurrection, God provided the only means of atonement for human sin, so that those who by faith accept this atonement may have eternal life, and the whole creation may better understand the infinite and holy love of the Creator. This perfect atonement vindicates the righteousness of God's law and the graciousness of His character; for it both condemns our sin and provides for our forgiveness. The death of Christ is substitutionary and expiatory, reconciling and transforming. The resurrection of Christ proclaims God's triumph over the forces of evil, and for those who accept the atonement assures their final victory over sin and death. It declares the Lordship of Jesus Christ, before whom every knee in heaven and on earth will bow.

(John 3:16; Isa. 53; 1 Pet. 2:21, 22; 1 Cor. 15:3, 4, 20–22; 2 Cor. 5:14, 15, 19–21; Rom. 1:4; 3:25; 4:25; 8:3, 4; 1 John 2:2; 4:10; Col. 2:15; Phil. 2:6–11.)

10. The Experience of Salvation

In infinite love and mercy God made Christ, who knew no sin, to be sin for us, so that in Him we might be made the righteousness of God. Led by the Holy Spirit we sense our need, acknowledge our sinfulness, repent of our transgressions, and exercise faith in Jesus as Lord and Christ, as Substitute and Example. This faith which receives salvation comes through the divine power of the Word and is the gift of God's grace. Through Christ we are justified, adopted as God's sons and daughters, and delivered from the lordship of sin. Through the Spirit we are born again and sanctified; the Spirit renews our minds, writes God's law of love in our hearts, and we are given the power to live a holy life. Abiding in Him we become partakers of the divine nature and have the assurance of salvation now and in the judgment.

(2 Cor. 5:17–21; John 3:16; Gal. 1:4; 4:4–7; Titus 3:3–7; John 16:8; Gal. 3:13, 14; 1 Pet. 2:21, 22; Rom. 10:17; Luke 17:5; Mark 9:23, 24; Eph. 2:5–10; Rom. 3:21–26; Col. 1:13, 14; Rom. 8:14–17; Gal. 3:26; John 3:3–8; 1 Pet. 1:23; Rom. 12:2; Heb. 8:7–12; Ezek. 36:25–27; 2 Pet. 1:3, 4; Rom. 8:1–4; 5:6–10.)

11. Growing in Christ

By His death on the cross Jesus triumphed over the forces of evil. He who subjugated the demonic spirits during His earthly ministry has broken their power and made certain their ultimate doom. Jesus' victory gives us victory over the evil forces that still seek to control us, as we walk with Him in peace, joy, and assurance of His love. Now the Holy Spirit dwells within us and empowers us. Continually committed to Jesus as our Saviour and Lord, we are set free from the burden of our past deeds. No longer do we live in the darkness, fear of evil powers, ignorance, and meaninglessness of our former way of life. In this new freedom in Jesus, we are called to grow into the likeness of His character, communing with Him daily in prayer, feeding on His Word, meditating on it and on His providence, singing His praises, gathering together for worship, and participating in the mission of the church. As we give ourselves in loving service to those around us and in witnessing to His salvation, His constant presence with us through the Spirit transforms every moment and every task into a spiritual experience.

(Pss. 1:1, 2; 23:4; 77:11, 12; Col. 1:13, 14; 2:6, 14, 15; Luke 10:17–20; Eph. 5:19, 20; 6:12–18; 1 Thess. 5:23; 2 Pet. 2:9; 3:18; 2 Cor. 3:17, 18; Phil. 3:7–14; 1 Thess. 5:16–18; Matt. 20:25–28; John 20:21; Gal. 5:22–25; Rom. 8:38, 39; 1 John 4:4; Heb. 10:25.)

12. The Church

The church is the community of believers who confess Jesus Christ as Lord and Saviour. In continuity with the people of God in Old Testament times, we are called out from the world; and we join together for worship, for fellowship, for instruction in the Word, for the celebration of the Lord's Supper, for service to all mankind, and for the worldwide proclamation of the gospel. The church derives its authority from Christ, who is the incarnate Word, and from the Scriptures, which are the written Word. The church is God's family; adopted by Him as children, its members live on the basis of the new covenant. The church is the body of Christ, a community of faith of which Christ Himself is the Head. The church is the bride for whom Christ died that He might sanctify and cleanse her. At His return in triumph, He will present her to Himself a glorious church, the faithful of all the ages, the purchase of His blood, not having spot or wrinkle, but holy and without blemish.

(Gen. 12:3; Acts 7:38; Eph. 4:11–15; 3:8–11; Matt. 28:19, 20; 16:13–20; 18:18; Eph. 2:19–22; 1:22, 23; 5:23–27; Col. 1:17, 18.)

13. The Remnant and Its Mission

The universal church is composed of all who truly believe in Christ, but in the last days, a time of widespread apostasy, a remnant has been called out to keep the commandments of God and the faith of Jesus. This remnant announces the arrival of the judgment hour, proclaims salvation through Christ, and heralds the approach of His second advent. This proclamation is symbolized by the three angels of Revelation 14; it coincides with the work of judgment in heaven and results in a work of repentance and reform on earth. Every believer is called to have a personal part in this worldwide witness.

(Rev. 12:17; 14:6–12; 18:1–4; 2 Cor. 5:10; Jude 3, 14; 1 Pet. 1:16–19; 2 Pet. 3:10–14; Rev. 21:1–14.)

14. Unity in the Body of Christ

The church is one body with many members, called from every nation, kindred, tongue, and people. In Christ we are a new creation; distinctions of race, culture, learning, and nationality, and differences between high and low, rich and poor, male and female, must not be divisive among us. We are all equal in Christ, who by one Spirit has bonded us into one fellowship with Him and with one another; we are to serve and be served without partiality or reservation. Through the revelation of Jesus Christ in the Scriptures we share the same faith and hope, and reach out in one witness to all. This unity has its source in the oneness of the triune God, who has adopted us as His children.

(Rom. 12:4, 5; 1 Cor. 12:12–14; Matt. 28:19, 20; Ps. 133:1; 2 Cor. 5:16, 17; Acts 17:26, 27; Gal. 3:27, 29; Col. 3:10–15; Eph. 4:14–16; 4:1–6; John 17:20–23.)

15. Baptism

By baptism we confess our faith in the death and resurrection of Jesus Christ, and testify of our death to sin and of our purpose to walk in newness of life. Thus we acknowledge Christ as Lord and Saviour, become His people, and are received as members by His church. Baptism is a symbol of our union with Christ, the forgiveness of our sins, and our reception of the Holy Spirit. It is by immersion in water and is contingent on an affirmation of faith in Jesus and evidence of repentance of sin. It follows instruction in the Holy Scriptures and acceptance of their teachings.

(Rom. 6:1–6; Col. 2:12, 13; Acts 16:30–33; 22:16; 2:38; Matt. 28:19, 20.)

16. The Lord's Supper

The Lord's Supper is a participation in the emblems of the body and blood of Jesus as an expression of faith in Him, our Lord and Saviour. In this experience of communion Christ is present to meet and strengthen His people. As we partake, we joyfully proclaim the Lord's death until He comes again. Preparation for the Supper includes self-examination, repentance, and confession. The Master ordained the service of foot washing to signify renewed cleansing, to express a willingness to serve one another in Christlike humility, and to unite our hearts in love. The communion service is open to all believing Christians.

(1 Cor. 10:16, 17; 11:23–30; Matt. 26:17–30; Rev. 3:20; John 6:48–63; 13:1–17.)

17. Spiritual Gifts and Ministries

God bestows upon all members of His church in every age spiritual gifts which each member is to employ in loving ministry for the common good of the church and of humanity. Given by the agency of the Holy Spirit, who apportions to each member as He wills, the gifts provide all abilities and ministries needed by the church to fulfill its divinely ordained functions. According to the Scriptures, these gifts include such ministries as faith, healing, prophecy, proclamation, teaching, administration, reconciliation, compassion, and self-sacrificing service and charity for the help and encouragement of people. Some members are called of God and endowed by the Spirit for functions recognized by the church in pastoral, evangelistic, apostolic, and teaching ministries particularly needed to equip the members for service, to build up the church to spiritual maturity, and to foster unity of the faith and knowledge of God. When members employ these spiritual gifts as faithful stewards of God's varied grace, the church is protected from the destructive influence of false doctrine, grows with a growth that is from God, and is built up in faith and love.

(Rom. 12:4–8; 1 Cor. 12:9–11, 27, 28; Eph. 4:8, 11–16; Acts 6:1–7; 1 Tim. 3:1–13; 1 Pet. 4:10, 11.)

18. The Gift of Prophecy

One of the gifts of the Holy Spirit is prophecy. This gift is an identifying mark of the remnant church and was manifested in the ministry of Ellen. G. White. As the Lord's messenger, her writings are a continuing and authoritative source of truth which provide for the church comfort, guidance, instruction, and correction. They also make clear that the Bible is the standard by which all teaching and experience must be tested.

(Joel 2:28, 29; Acts 2:14–21; Heb. 1:1–3; Rev. 12:17; 19:10.)

19. The Law of God

The great principles of God's law are embodied in the Ten Commandments and exemplified in the life of Christ. They express God's love, will, and purposes concerning human conduct and relationships and are binding upon all people in every age. These precepts are the basis of God's covenant with His people and the standard in God's judgment. Through the agency of the Holy Spirit they point out sin and awaken a sense of need for a Saviour. Salvation is all of grace and not of works, but its fruitage is obedience to the Commandments. This obedience develops Christian character and results in a sense of well-being. It is an evidence of our love for the Lord and our concern for our fellow men. The obedience of faith demonstrates the power of Christ to transform lives, and therefore strengthens Christian witness.

(Exod. 20:1–17; Ps. 40:7, 8; Matt. 22:36–40; Deut. 28:1–14; Matt. 5:17–20; Heb. 8:8–10; John 15:7–10; Eph. 2:8–10; 1 John 5:3; Rom. 8:3, 4; Ps. 19:7–14.)

20. The Sabbath

The beneficent Creator, after the six days of Creation, rested on the seventh day and instituted the Sabbath for all people as a memorial of Creation. The fourth commandment of God's unchangeable law requires the observance of this seventh-day Sabbath as the day of rest, worship, and ministry in harmony with the teaching and practice of Jesus, the Lord of the Sabbath. The Sabbath is a day of delightful communion with God and one another. It is a symbol of our redemption in Christ, a sign of our sanctification, a token of our allegiance, and a foretaste of our eternal future in God's kingdom. The Sabbath is God's perpetual sign of His eternal covenant between Him and His people. Joyful observance of this holy time from evening to evening, sunset to sunset, is a celebration of God's creative and redemptive acts.

(Gen. 2:1–3; Exod. 20:8–11; Luke 4:16; Isa. 56:5, 6; 58:13, 14; Matt. 12:1–12; Exod. 31:13–17; Ezek. 20:12, 20; Deut. 5:12–15; Heb. 4:1–11; Lev. 23:32; Mark 1:32.)

21. Stewardship

We are God's stewards, entrusted by Him with time and opportunities, abilities and possessions, and the blessings of the earth and its resources. We are responsible to Him for their proper use. We acknowledge God's ownership by faithful service to Him and our fellow men, and by returning tithes and giving offerings for the proclamation of His gospel and the support and growth of His church. Stewardship is a privilege given to us by God for nurture in love and the victory over selfishness and covetousness. The steward rejoices in the blessings that come to others as a result of his faithfulness.

(Gen. 1:26–28; 2:15; 1 Chron. 29:14; Hag. 1:3–11; Mal. 3:8–12; 1 Cor. 9:9–14; Matt. 23:23; 2 Cor. 8:1–15; Rom. 15:26, 27.)

22. Christian Behavior

We are called to be a godly people who think, feel, and act in harmony with the principles of heaven. For the Spirit to recreate in us the character of our Lord we involve ourselves only in those things which will produce Christlike purity, health, and joy in our lives. This means that our amusement and entertainment should meet the highest standards of Christian taste and beauty. While recognizing cultural differences, our dress is to be simple, modest, and neat, befitting those whose true beauty does not consist of outward adornment but in the imperishable ornament of a gentle and quiet spirit. It also means that because our bodies are the temples of the Holy Spirit, we are to care for them intelligently. Along with adequate exercise and rest, we are to adopt the most healthful diet possible and abstain from the unclean foods identified in the Scriptures. Since alcoholic beverages, tobacco, and the irresponsible use of drugs and narcotics are harmful to our bodies, we are to abstain from them as well. Instead, we are to engage in whatever brings our thoughts and bodies into the discipline of Christ, who desires our wholesomeness, joy, and goodness.

(Rom. 12:1, 2; 1 John 2:6; Eph. 5:1–21; Phil. 4:8; 2 Cor. 10:5; 6:14–7:1; 1 Pet. 3:1–4; 1 Cor. 6:19, 20; 10:31; Lev. 11:1–47; 3 John 2.)

23. Marriage and the Family

Marriage was divinely established in Eden and affirmed by Jesus to be a lifelong union between a man and a woman in loving companionship. For the Christian a marriage commitment is to God as well as to the spouse, and should be entered into only between partners who share a common faith. Mutual love, honor, respect, and responsibility are the fabric of this relationship, which is to reflect the love, sanctity, closeness, and permanence of the relationship between Christ and His church. Regarding divorce, Jesus taught that the person who divorces a spouse, except for fornication, and marries another, commits adultery. Although some family relationships may fall short of the ideal, marriage partners who fully commit themselves to each other in Christ may achieve loving unity through the guidance of the Spirit and the nurture of the church. God blesses the family and intends that its members shall assist each other toward complete maturity. Parents are to bring up their children to love and obey the Lord. By their example and their words they are to teach them that Christ is a loving disciplinarian, ever tender and caring, who wants them to become members of His body, the family of God. Increasing family closeness is one of the earmarks of the final gospel message.

(Gen. 2:18–25; Matt. 19:3–9; John 2:1–11; 2 Cor. 6:14; Eph. 5:21–33; Matt. 5:31, 32; Mark 10:11, 12; Luke 16:18; 1 Cor. 7:10, 11; Exod. 20:12; Eph. 6:1–4; Deut. 6:5–9; Prov. 22:6; Mal. 4:5, 6.)

24. Christ's Ministry in the Heavenly Sanctuary

There is a sanctuary in heaven, the true tabernacle which the Lord set up and not man. In it Christ ministers on our behalf, making available to believers the benefits of His atoning sacrifice offered once for all on the cross. He was inaugurated as our great High Priest and began His intercessory ministry at the time of His ascension. In 1844, at the end of the prophetic period of 2300 days, He entered the second and last phase of His atoning ministry. It is a work of investigative judgment which is part of the ultimate disposition of all sin, typified by the cleansing of the ancient Hebrew sanctuary on the Day of Atonement. In that typical service the sanctuary was cleansed with the blood of animal sacrifices, but the heavenly things are purified with the perfect sacrifice of the blood of Jesus. The investigative judgment reveals to heavenly intelligences who among the dead are asleep in Christ and therefore, in Him, are deemed worthy to have part in the first resurrection. It also makes manifest who among the living are abiding in Christ, keeping the commandments of God and the faith of Jesus, and in Him, therefore, are ready for translation into His everlasting kingdom. This judgment vindicates the justice of God in saving those who believe in Jesus. It declares that those who have remained loyal to God shall receive the kingdom. The completion of this ministry of Christ will mark the close of human probation before the Second Advent.

(Heb. 8:1–5; 4:14–16; 9:11–28; 10:19–22; 1:3; 2:16, 17; Dan. 7:9–27; 8:13, 14; 9:24–27; Num. 14:34; Ezek. 4:6; Lev. 16; Rev. 14:6, 7; 20:12; 14:12; 22:12.)

25. The Second Coming of Christ

The second coming of Christ is the blessed hope of the church, the grand climax of the gospel. The Saviour's coming will be literal, personal, visible, and worldwide. When He returns, the righteous dead will be resurrected, and together with the righteous living will be glorified and taken to heaven, but the unrighteous will die. The almost complete fulfillment of most lines of prophecy, together with the present condition of the world, indicates that Christ's coming is imminent. The time of that event has not been revealed, and we are therefore exhorted to be ready at all times.

(Titus 2:13; Heb. 9:28; John 14:1–3; Acts 1:9–11; Matt. 24:14; Rev. 1:7; Matt. 24:43, 44; 1 Thess. 4:13–18; 1 Cor. 15:51–54; 2 Thess. 1:7–10; 2:8; Rev. 14:14–20; 19:11–21; Matt. 24; Mark 13; Luke 21; 2 Tim. 3:1-5; 1 Thess. 5:1–6.)

26. Death and Resurrection

The wages of sin is death. But God, who alone is immortal, will grant eternal life to His redeemed. Until that day death is an unconscious state for all people. When Christ, who is our life, appears, the resurrected righteous and the living righteous will be glorified and caught up to meet their Lord. The second resurrection, the resurrection of the unrighteous, will take place a thousand years later.

(Rom. 6:23; 1 Tim. 6:15, 16; Eccles. 9:5, 6; Ps. 146:3, 4; John 11:11–14; Col. 3:4; 1 Cor. 15:51–54; 1 Thess. 4:13–17; John 5:28, 29; Rev. 20:1–10.)

27. The Millennium and the End of Sin

The millennium is the thousand-year reign of Christ with His saints in heaven between the first and second resurrections. During this time the wicked dead will be judged; the earth will be utterly desolate, without living human inhabitants, but occupied by Satan and his angels. At its close Christ with His saints and the Holy City will descend from heaven to earth. The unrighteous dead will then be resurrected, and with Satan and his angels will surround the city; but fire from God will consume them and cleanse the earth. The universe will thus be freed of sin and sinners forever.

(Rev. 20; 1 Cor. 6:2, 3; Jer. 4:23–26; Rev. 21:1–5; Mal. 4:1; Ezek. 28:18, 19.)

28. The New Earth

On the new earth, in which righteousness dwells, God will provide an eternal home for the redeemed and a perfect environment for everlasting life, love, joy, and learning in His presence. For here God Himself will dwell with His people, and suffering and death will have passed away. The great controversy will be ended, and sin will be no more. All things, animate and inanimate, will declare that God is love; and He shall reign forever. Amen.

(2 Pet. 3:13; Isa. 35; 65:17–25; Matt. 5:5; Rev. 21:1–7; 22:1–5; 11:15.)